HEATHCLIFF

GHOSTS, GOBLINS
AND CREEPY THINGS LIKE THAT

by Geo Gately

TOR

A TOM DOHERTY ASSOCIATES BOOK
NEW YORK

This is a work of fiction. All the characters and events portrayed in this book are fictitious, and any resemblance to real people or events is purely coincidental.

HEATHCLIFF®: GHOSTS, GOBLINS AND CREEPY THINGS LIKE THAT

Originally published by Marvel Comics in magazine form as HEATHCLIFF #10, #13, and #32 and FUNHOUSE #3 and #10

A Tor Book
Published by Tom Doherty Associates, Inc.
49 West 24th Street
New York, N.Y. 10010

ISBN: 0-812-50990-0

First printing: October 1990

Printed in the United States of America

0 9 8 7 6 5 4 3 2 1

ACKNOWLEDGMENTS

The Haunted Lighthouse — *Angelo DeCesare, writer; Warren Kremer, penciler; Jacqueline Roettcher, inker*

Fright Day at the Bijou—*Angelo DeCesare, writer; Warren Kremer, penciler; Jacqueline Roettcher, inker*

A Horrible Little Shop—*Laura Hitchcock, writer; Howard Post, penciler; Jacqueline Roettcher, inker*

Which Mouse is Witch — *Michael Gallagher, writer; Warren Kremer, penciler; Ruth Leon, inker*

The Werewolf of Westfinster—*Michael Gallagher, writer; Warren Kremer, penciler; Jacqueline Roettcher, inker*

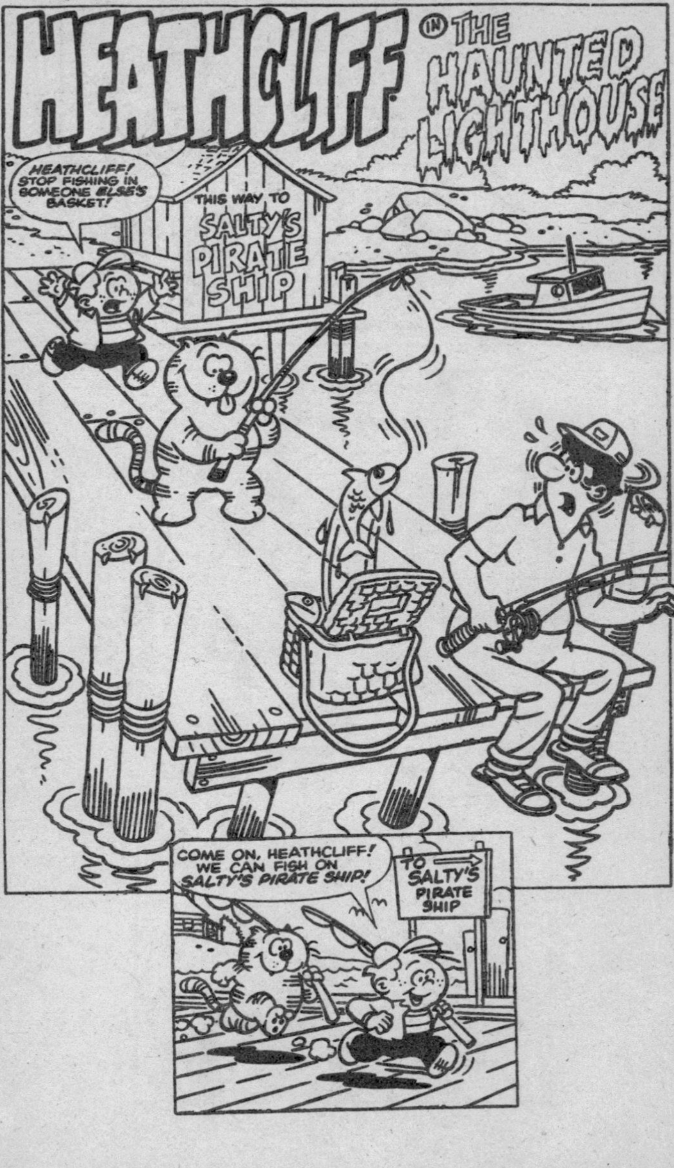
HEATHCLIFF
IN THE HAUNTED LIGHTHOUSE
HEATHCLIFF! STOP FISHING IN SOMEONE ELSE'S BASKET!
THIS WAY TO SALTY'S PIRATE SHIP
COME ON, HEATHCLIFF! WE CAN FISH ON SALTY'S PIRATE SHIP!
TO SALTY'S PIRATE SHIP

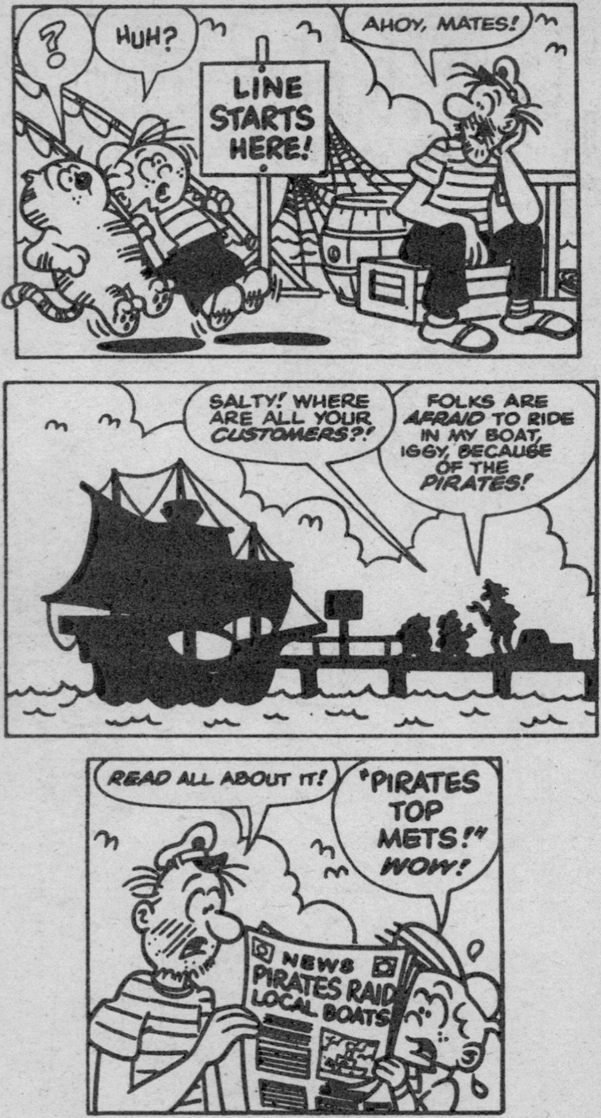
?
HUH?
LINE STARTS HERE!
AHOY, MATES!
SALTY! WHERE ARE ALL YOUR CUSTOMERS?!
FOLKS ARE AFRAID TO RIDE IN MY BOAT, IGGY, BECAUSE OF THE PIRATES!
READ ALL ABOUT IT!
"PIRATES TOP METS!" WOW!
NEWS
PIRATES RAID LOCAL BOATS

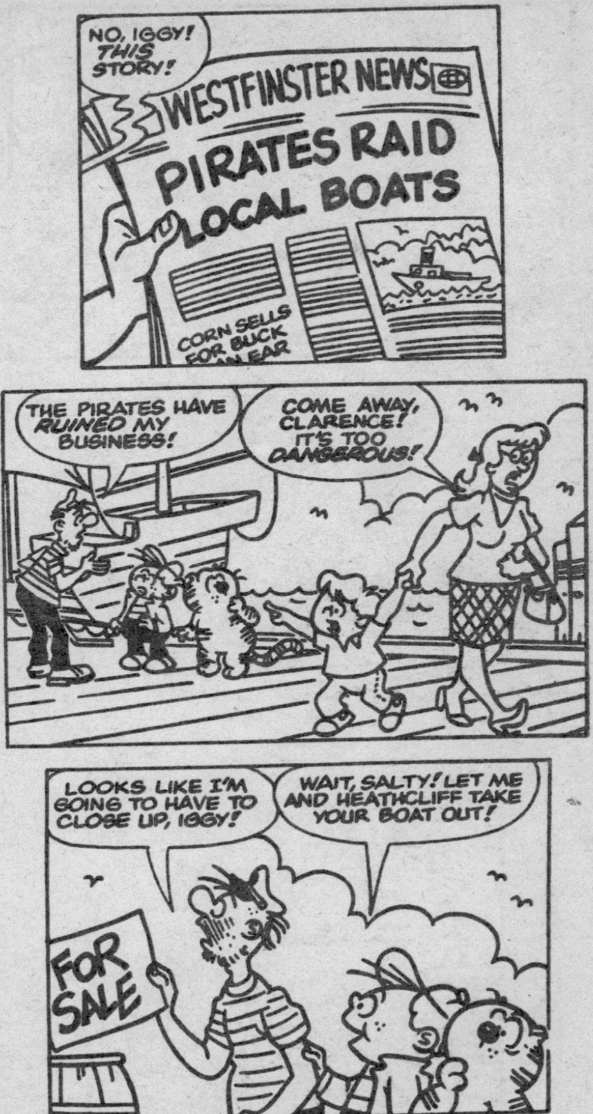
NO, IGGY! *THIS* STORY!
WESTFINSTER NEWS
PIRATES RAID LOCAL BOATS
CORN SELLS FOR BUCK
THE PIRATES HAVE *RUINED* MY BUSINESS!
COME AWAY, CLARENCE! IT'S TOO *DANGEROUS!*
LOOKS LIKE I'M GOING TO HAVE TO CLOSE UP, IGGY!
WAIT, SALTY! LET ME AND HEATHCLIFF TAKE YOUR BOAT OUT!
FOR SALE

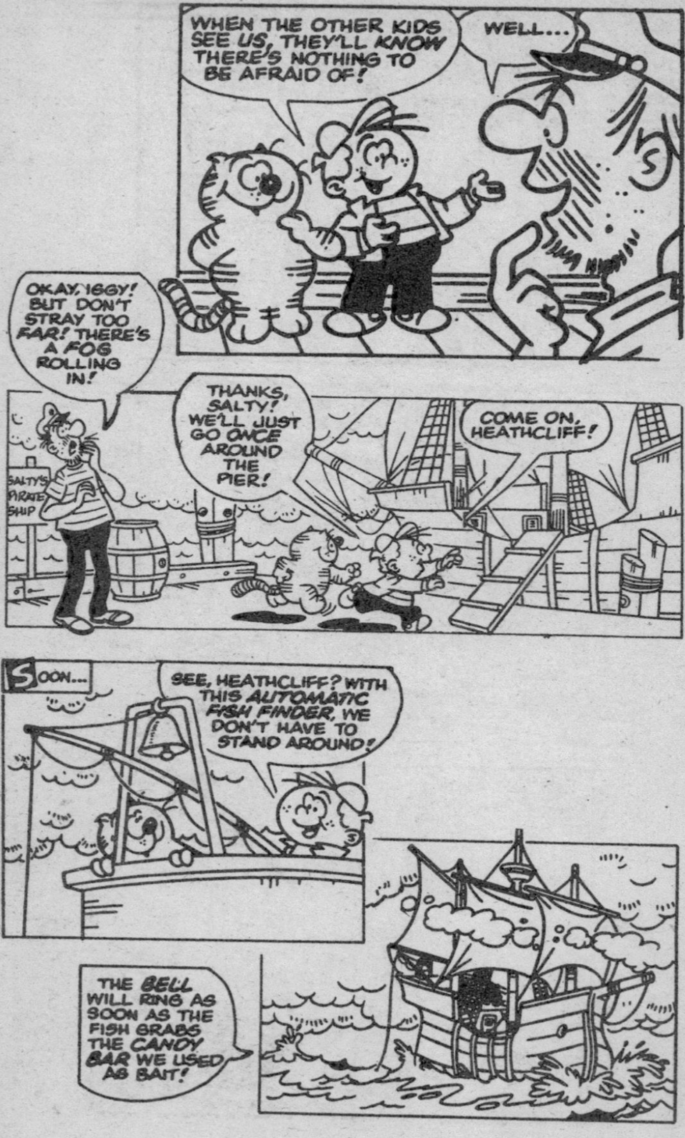
WHEN THE OTHER KIDS SEE US, THEY'LL KNOW THERE'S NOTHING TO BE AFRAID OF!
WELL...
OKAY, IGGY! BUT DON'T STRAY TOO FAR! THERE'S A FOG ROLLING IN!
THANKS, SALTY! WE'LL JUST GO ONCE AROUND THE PIER!
COME ON, HEATHCLIFF!
SALTY'S PIRATE SHIP
SOON...
SEE, HEATHCLIFF? WITH THIS AUTOMATIC FISH FINDER, WE DON'T HAVE TO STAND AROUND!
THE BELL WILL RING AS SOON AS THE FISH GRABS THE CANDY BAR WE USED AS BAIT!

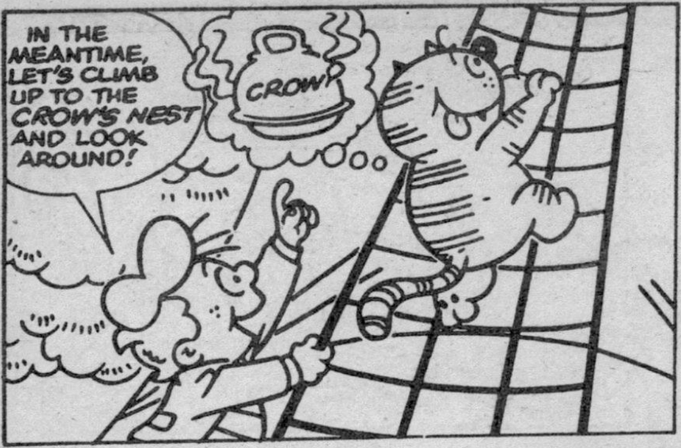
IN THE MEANTIME, LET'S CLIMB UP TO THE CROW'S NEST AND LOOK AROUND!
CROW

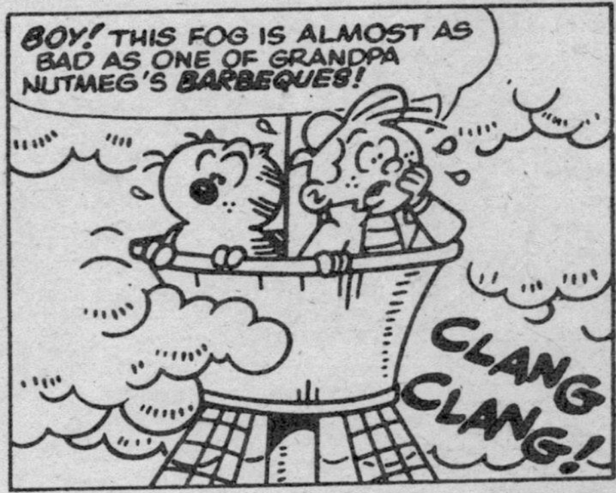
BOY! THIS FOG IS ALMOST AS BAD AS ONE OF GRANDPA NUTMEG'S BARBEQUES!
CLANG CLANG!

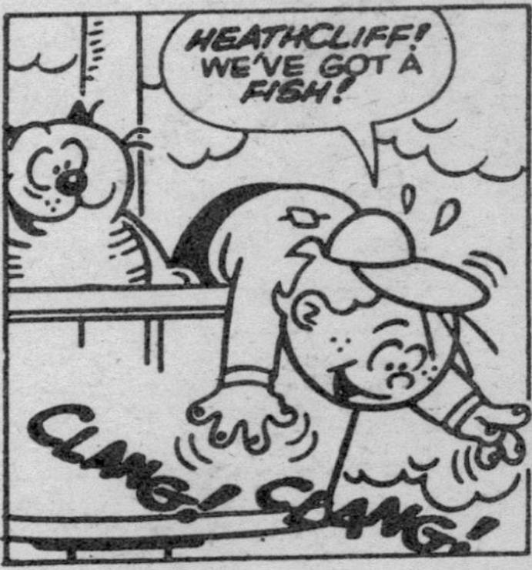
HEATHCLIFF! WE'VE GOT A FISH!
CLANG! CLANG!

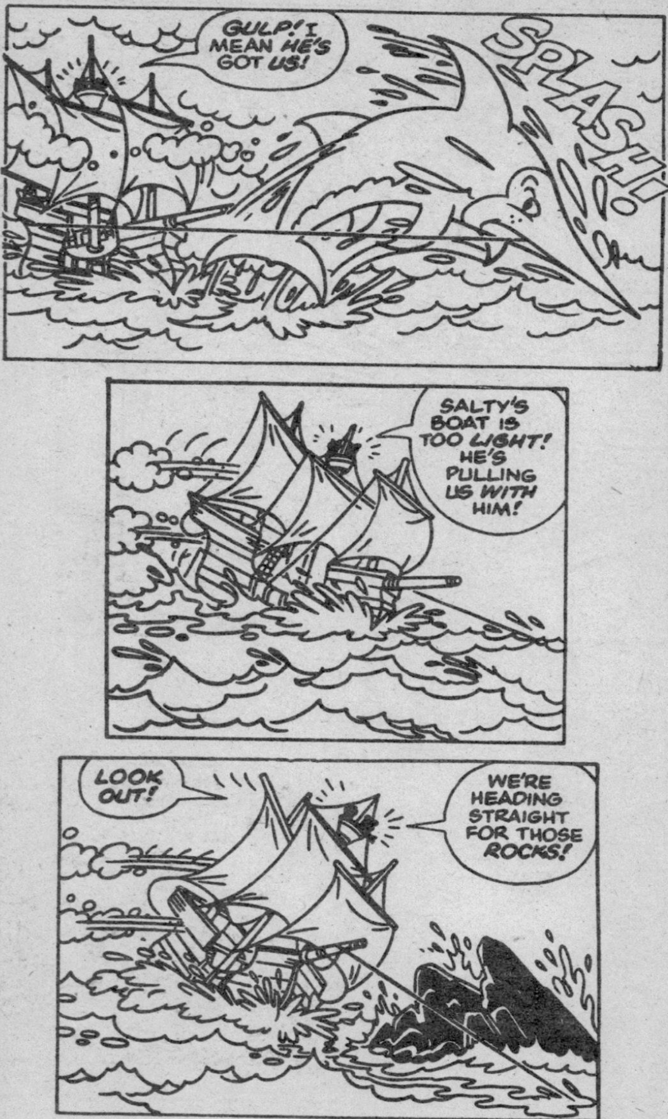
GULP! I MEAN HE'S GOT US!
SPLASH!
SALTY'S BOAT IS TOO LIGHT! HE'S PULLING US WITH HIM!
LOOK OUT!
WE'RE HEADING STRAIGHT FOR THOSE ROCKS!

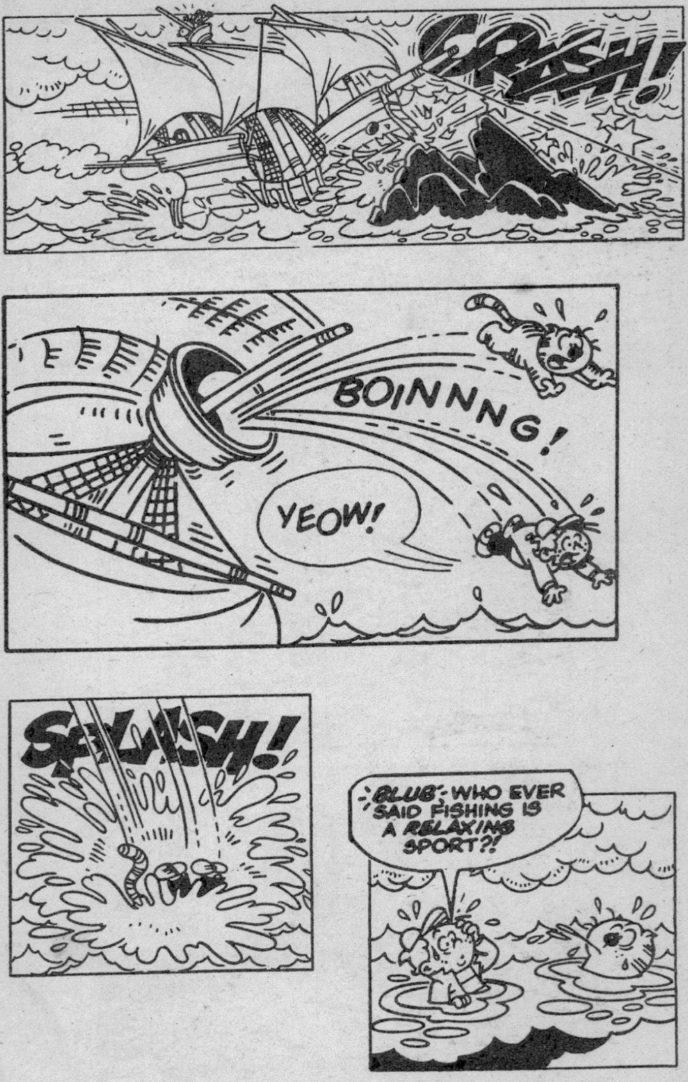
CRASH!
BOINNNNG!
YEOW!
SPLASH!
BLUB - WHO EVER SAID FISHING IS A RELAXING SPORT?!

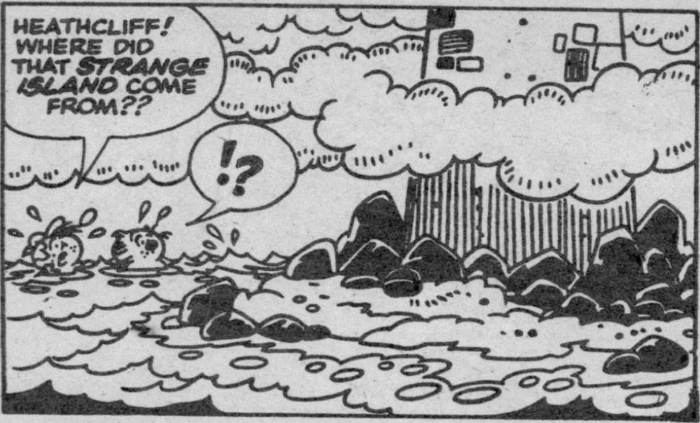
HEATHCLIFF! WHERE DID THAT STRANGE ISLAND COME FROM??
!?

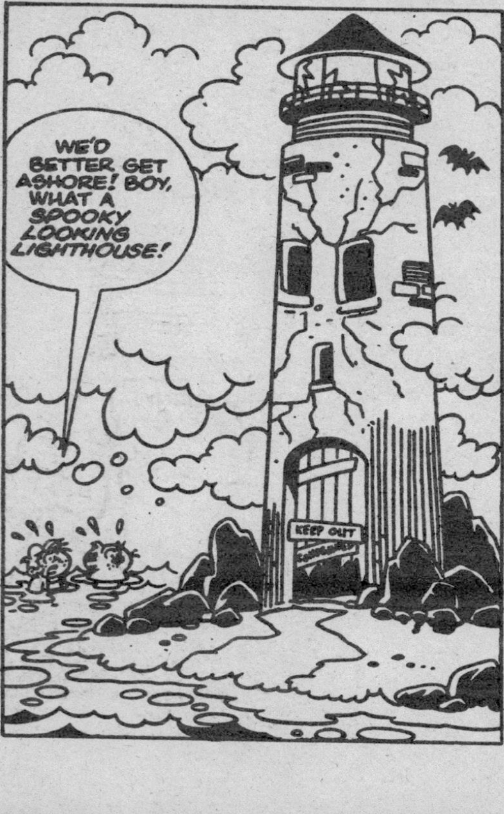
WE'D BETTER GET ASHORE! BOY, WHAT A SPOOKY LOOKING LIGHTHOUSE!
KEEP OUT

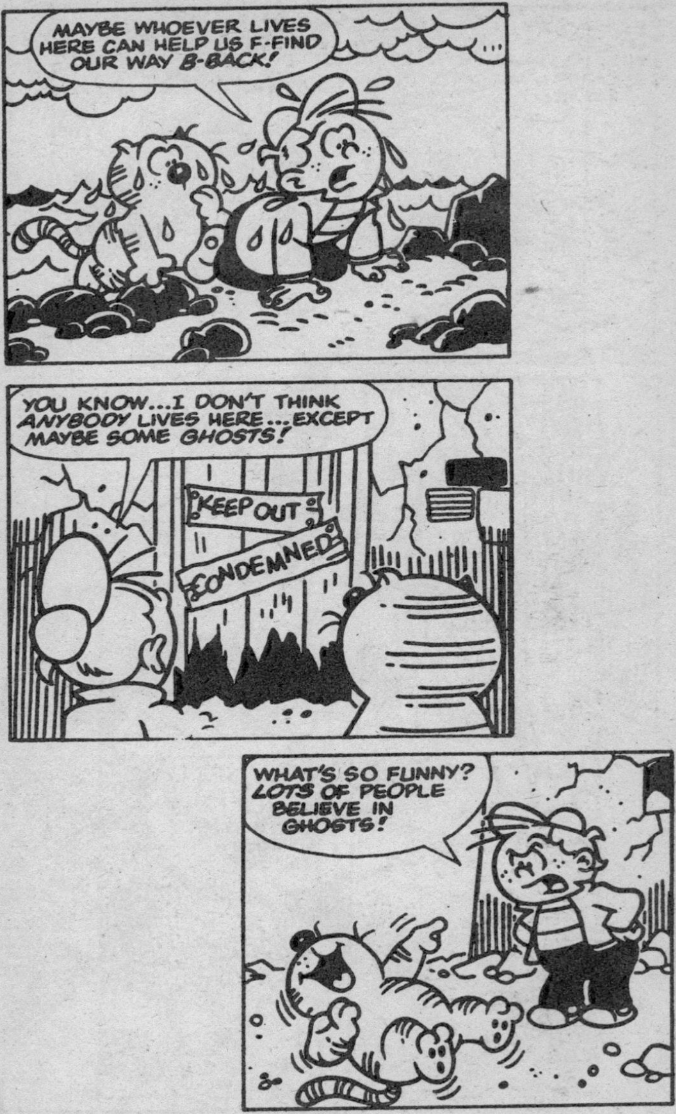
MAYBE WHOEVER LIVES HERE CAN HELP US F-FIND OUR WAY B-BACK!
YOU KNOW...I DON'T THINK ANYBODY LIVES HERE...EXCEPT MAYBE SOME GHOSTS!
KEEP OUT
CONDEMNED
WHAT'S SO FUNNY? LOTS OF PEOPLE BELIEVE IN GHOSTS!

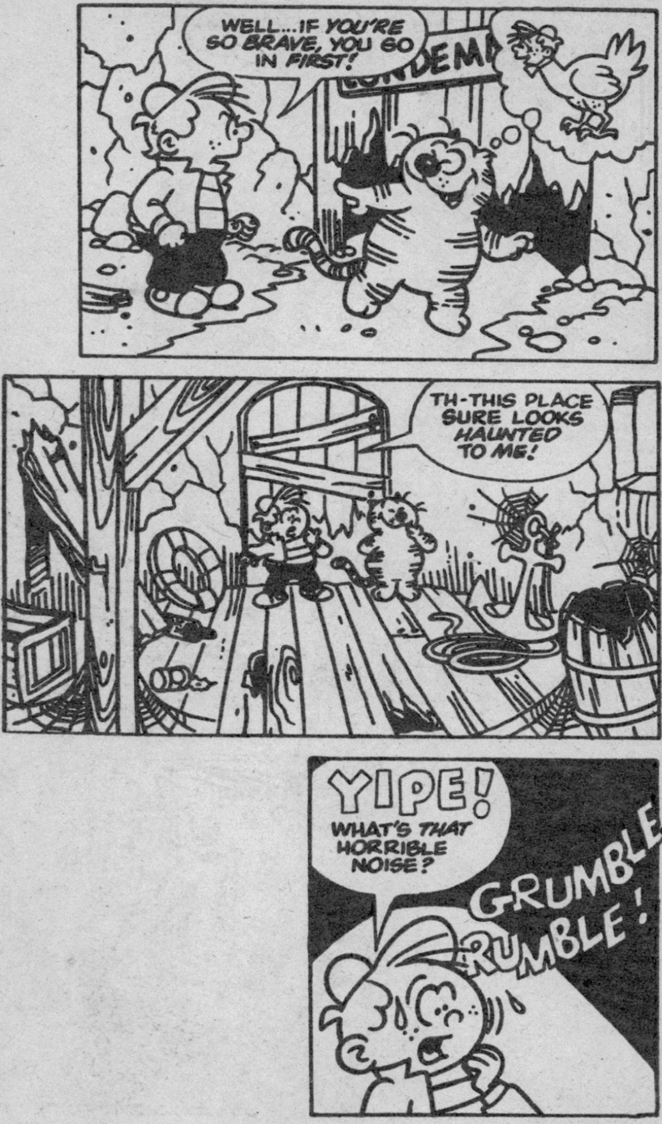
WELL...IF YOU'RE SO BRAVE, YOU GO IN FIRST!
CONDEM
TH-THIS PLACE SURE LOOKS HAUNTED TO ME!
YIPE! WHAT'S THAT HORRIBLE NOISE?
GRUMBLE RUMBLE!

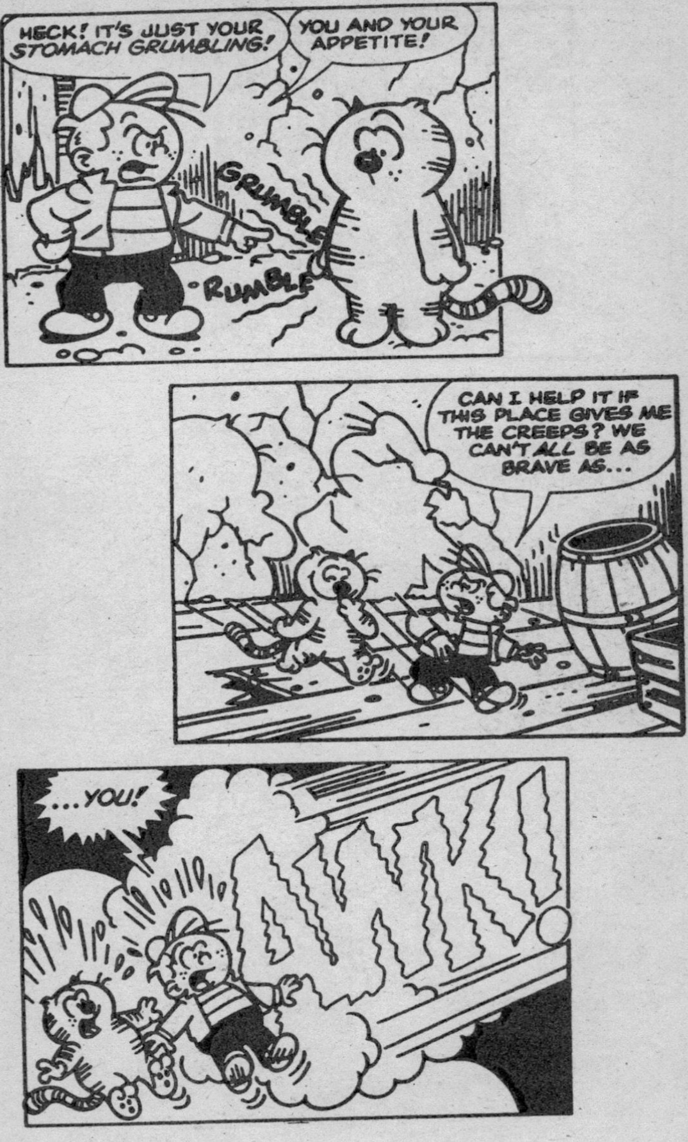
HECK! IT'S JUST YOUR STOMACH GRUMBLING!
YOU AND YOUR APPETITE!
GRUMBLE
RUMBLE
CAN I HELP IT IF THIS PLACE GIVES ME THE CREEPS? WE CAN'T ALL BE AS BRAVE AS...
...YOU!

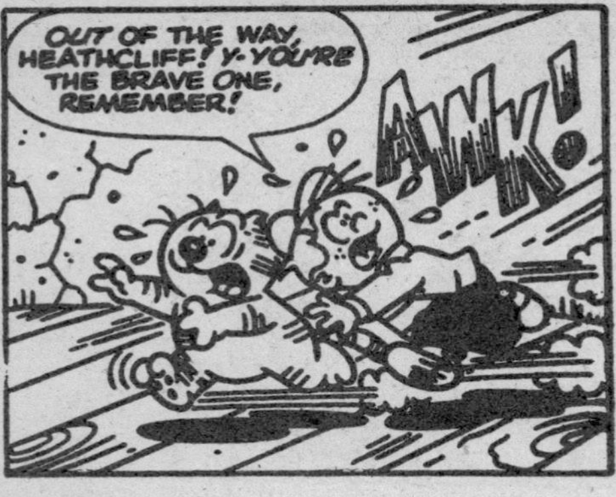
OUT OF THE WAY, HEATHCLIFF! Y-YOU'RE THE BRAVE ONE, REMEMBER!
AWK!

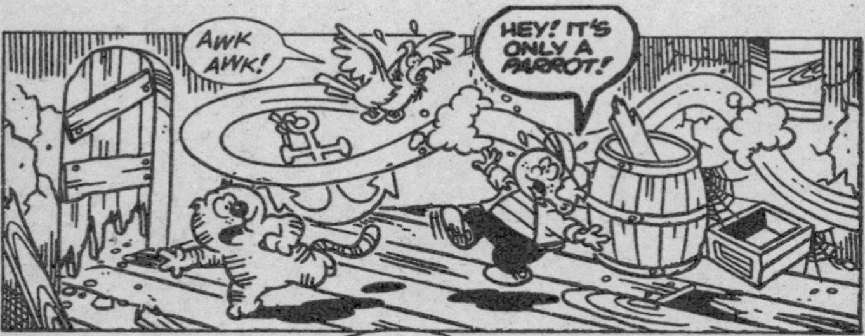
AWK AWK!
HEY! IT'S ONLY A PARROT!

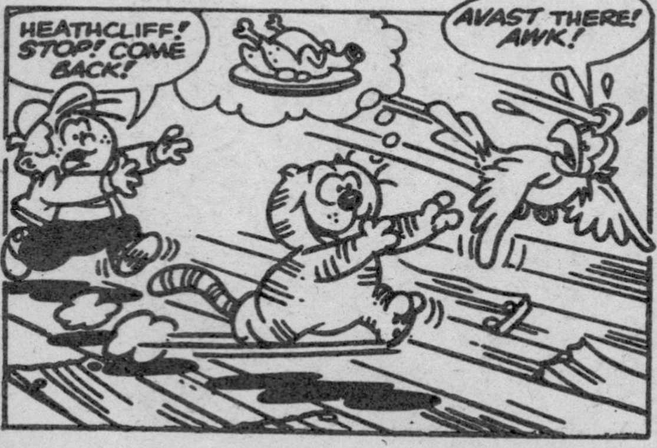
HEATHCLIFF! STOP! COME BACK!
AVAST THERE! AWK!

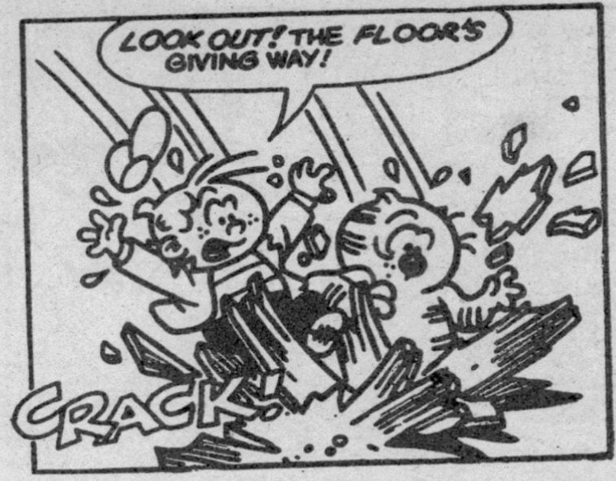
LOOK OUT! THE FLOOR'S GIVING WAY!
CRACK!

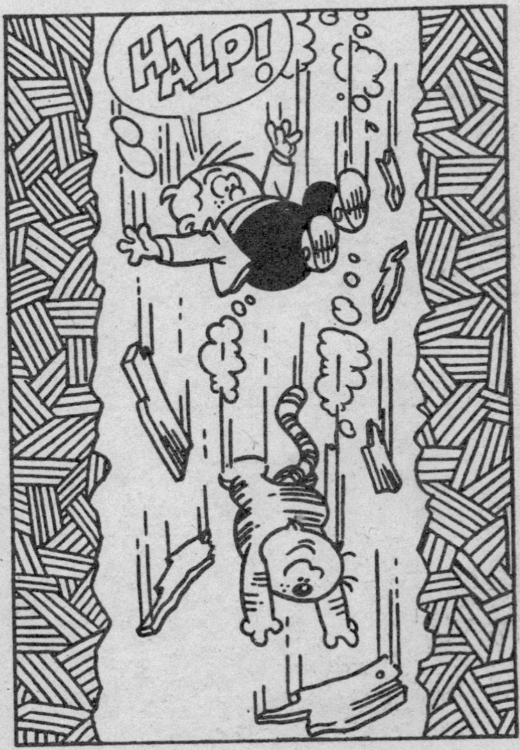
HALP!

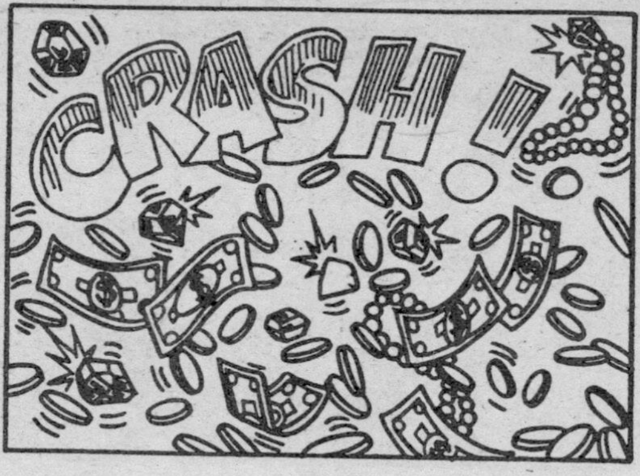
CRASH!

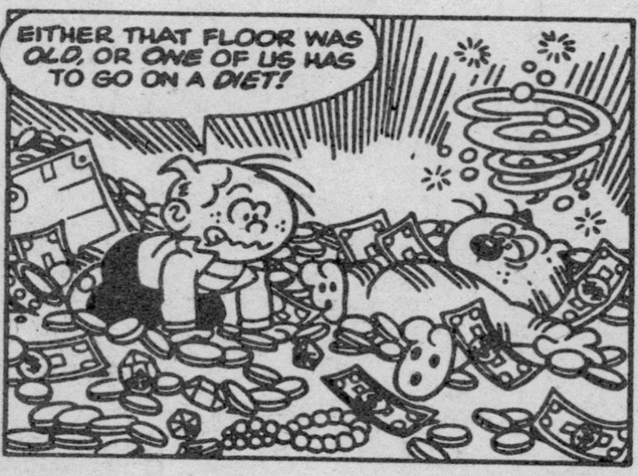
EITHER THAT FLOOR WAS OLD, OR ONE OF US HAS TO GO ON A DIET!

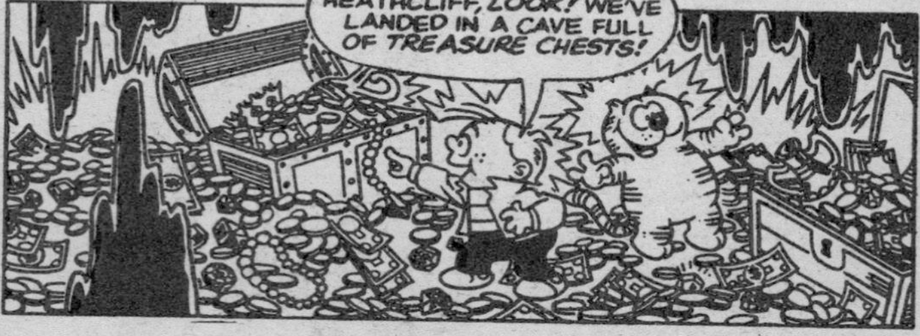
HEATHCLIFF, LOOK! WE'VE LANDED IN A CAVE FULL OF TREASURE CHESTS!

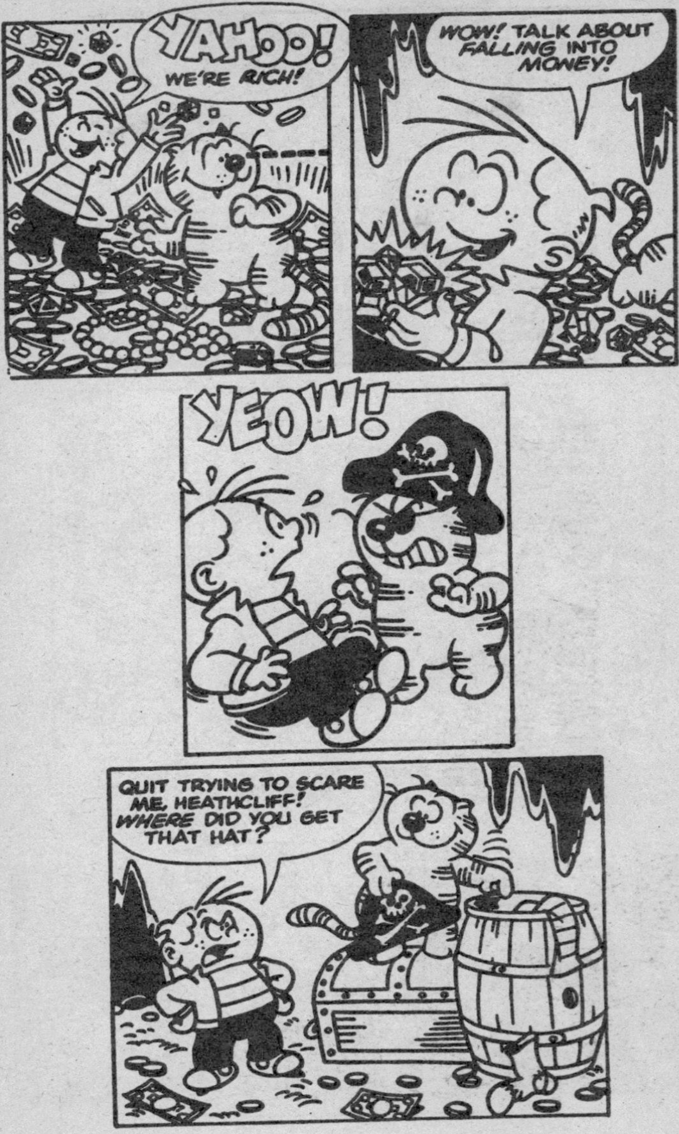
YAHOO!
WE'RE RICH!
WOW! TALK ABOUT FALLING INTO MONEY!
YEOW!
QUIT TRYING TO SCARE ME, HEATHCLIFF! WHERE DID YOU GET THAT HAT?

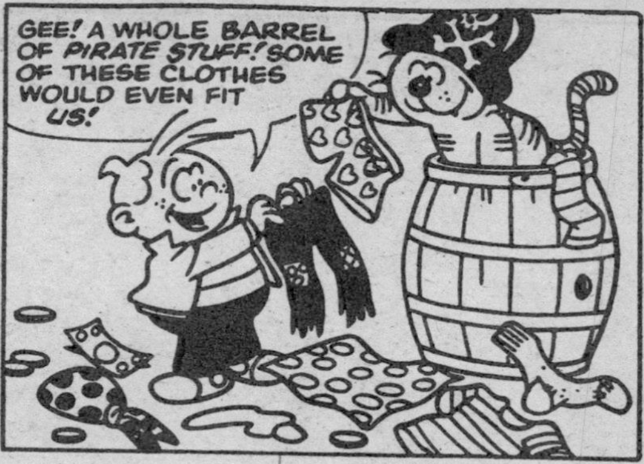
GEE! A WHOLE BARREL OF PIRATE STUFF! SOME OF THESE CLOTHES WOULD EVEN FIT US!

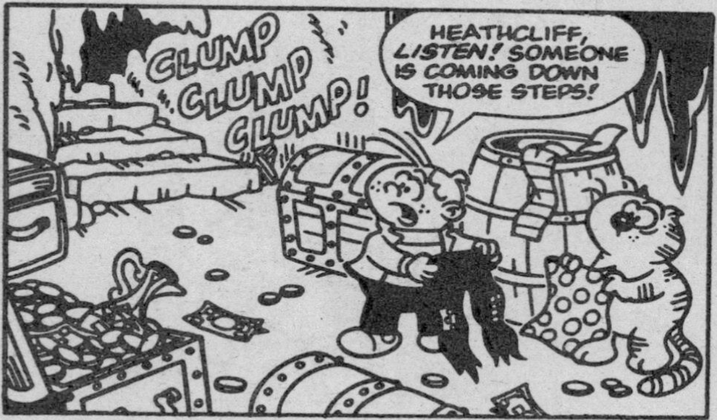
CLUMP
CLUMP
CLUMP!
HEATHCLIFF, LISTEN! SOMEONE IS COMING DOWN THOSE STEPS!

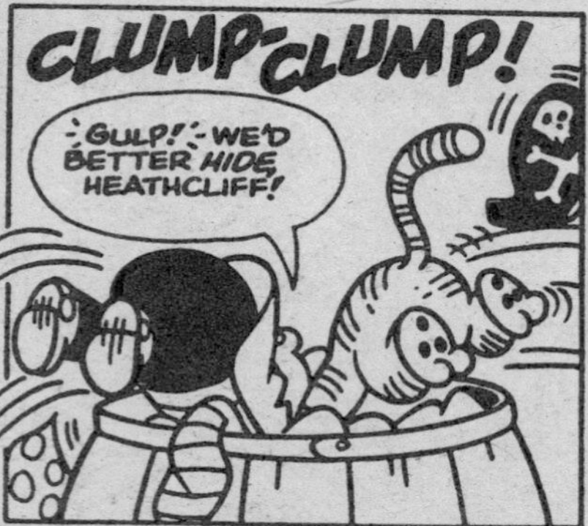
CLUMP-CLUMP!
-GULP!- WE'D BETTER HIDE, HEATHCLIFF!

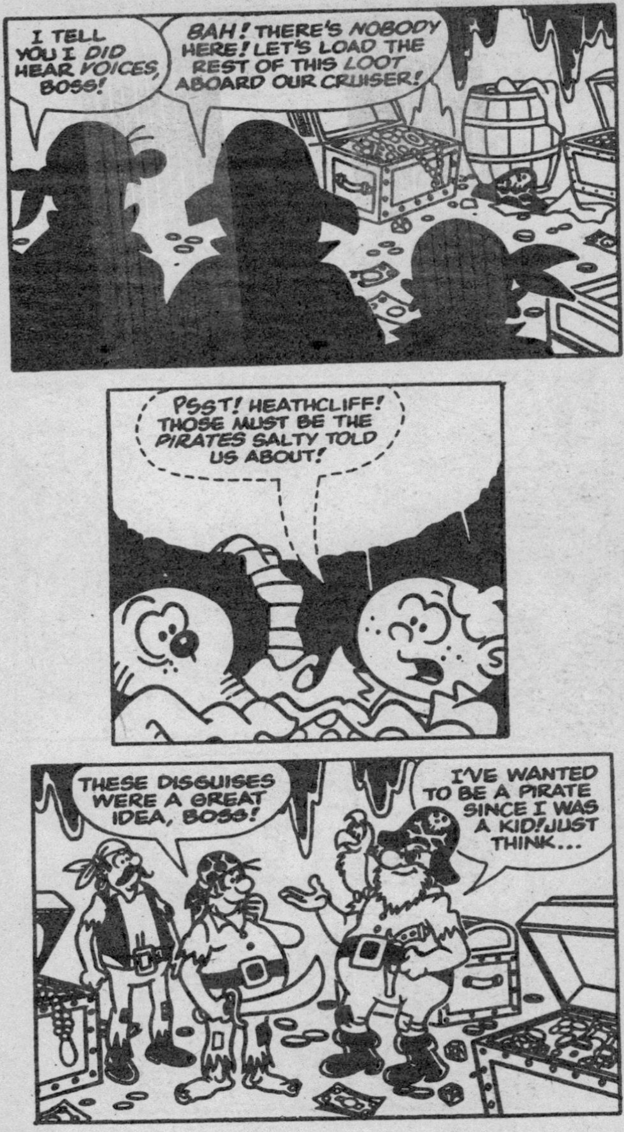
I TELL YOU I DID HEAR VOICES, BOSS!
BAH! THERE'S NOBODY HERE! LET'S LOAD THE REST OF THIS LOOT ABOARD OUR CRUISER!
PSST! HEATHCLIFF! THOSE MUST BE THE PIRATES SALTY TOLD US ABOUT!
THESE DISGUISES WERE A GREAT IDEA, BOSS!
I'VE WANTED TO BE A PIRATE SINCE I WAS A KID! JUST THINK...

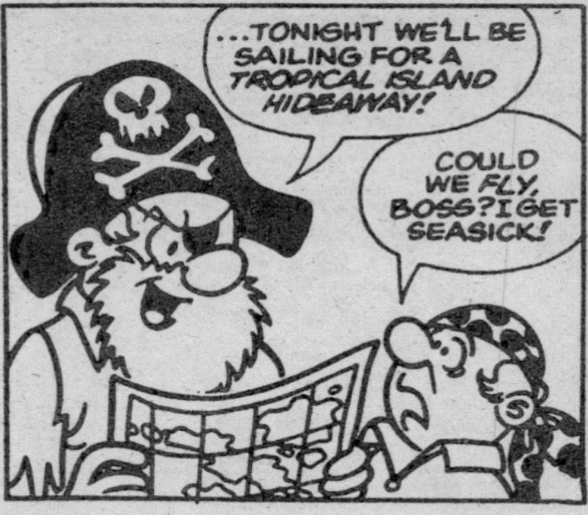
...TONIGHT WE'LL BE SAILING FOR A TROPICAL ISLAND HIDEAWAY!
COULD WE FLY, BOSS? I GET SEASICK!

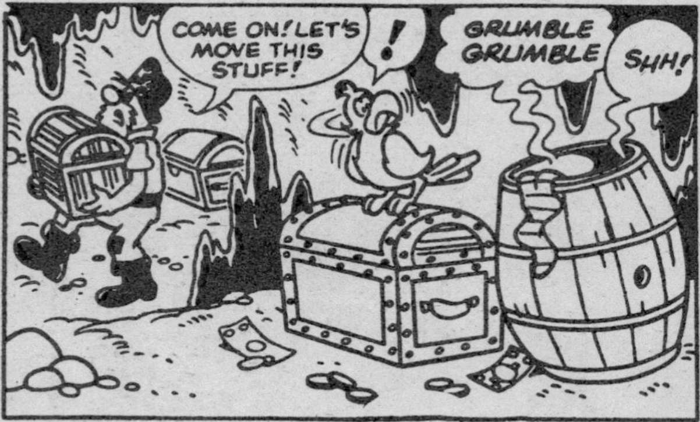
COME ON! LET'S MOVE THIS STUFF!
!
GRUMBLE GRUMBLE
SHH!

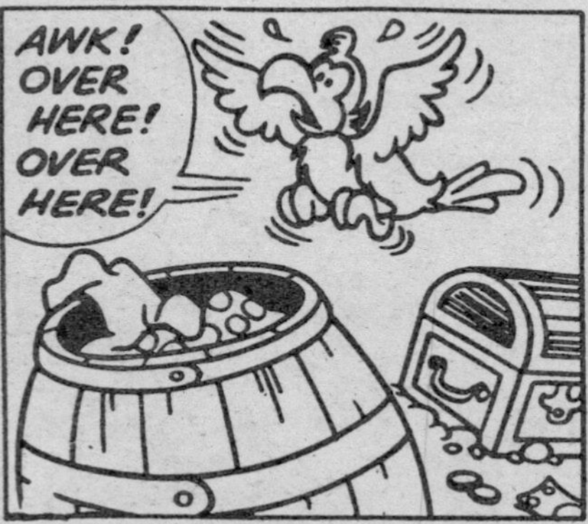
AWK! OVER HERE! OVER HERE!

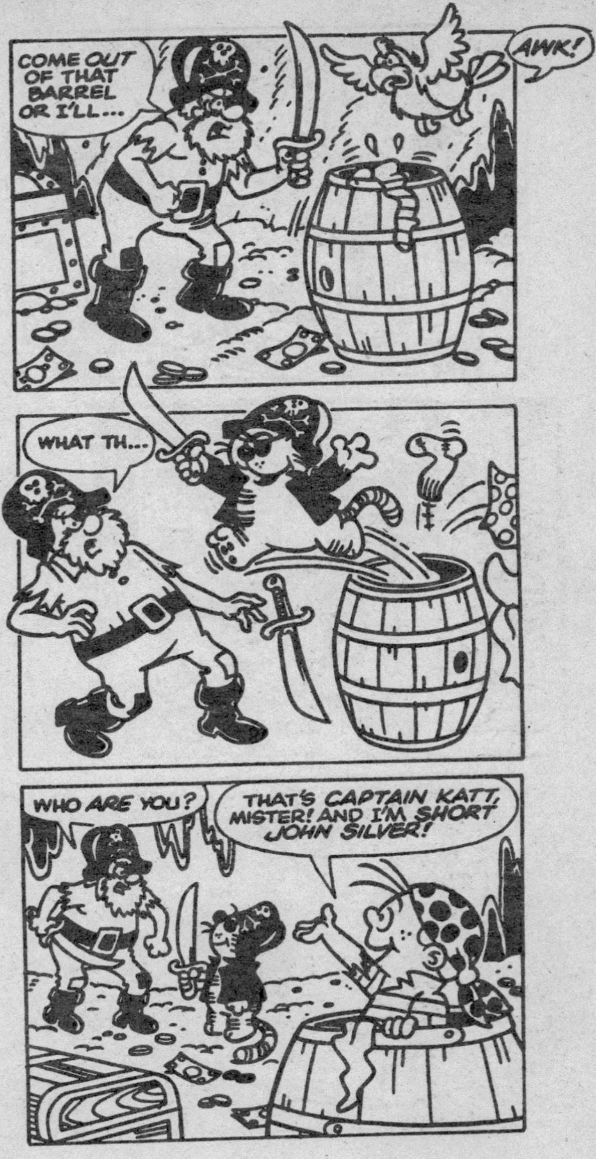
COME OUT OF THAT BARREL OR I'LL...
AWK!
WHAT TH...
WHO ARE YOU?
THAT'S CAPTAIN KATT, MISTER! AND I'M SHORT JOHN SILVER!

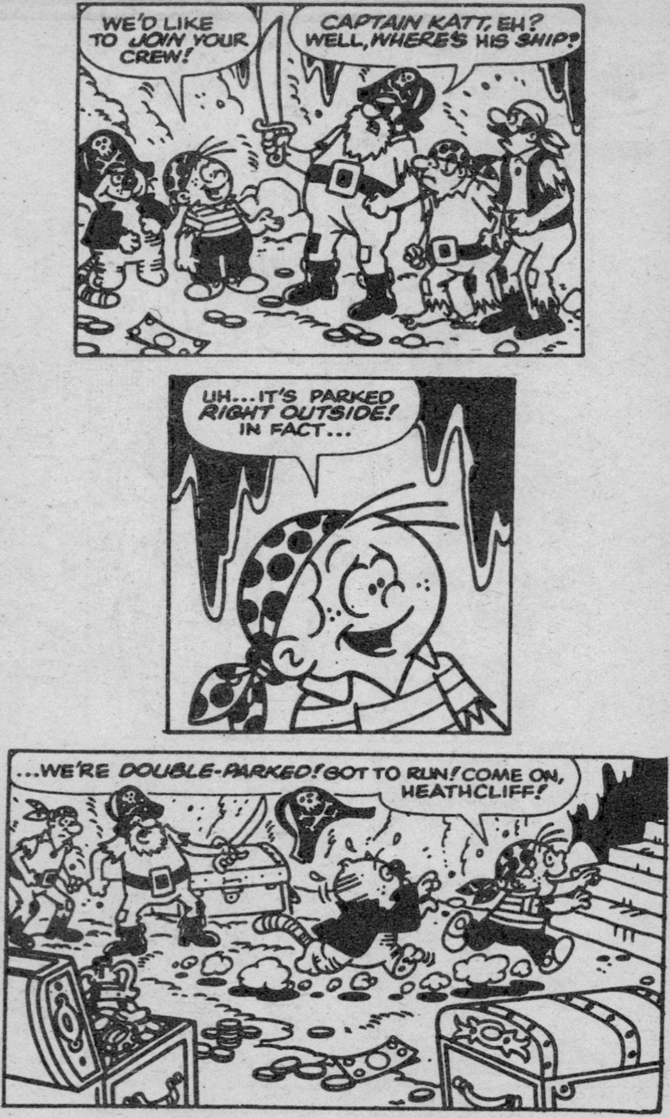
WE'D LIKE TO JOIN YOUR CREW!
CAPTAIN KATT, EH? WELL, WHERE'S HIS SHIP?
UH... IT'S PARKED RIGHT OUTSIDE! IN FACT...
...WE'RE DOUBLE-PARKED! GOT TO RUN! COME ON, HEATHCLIFF!

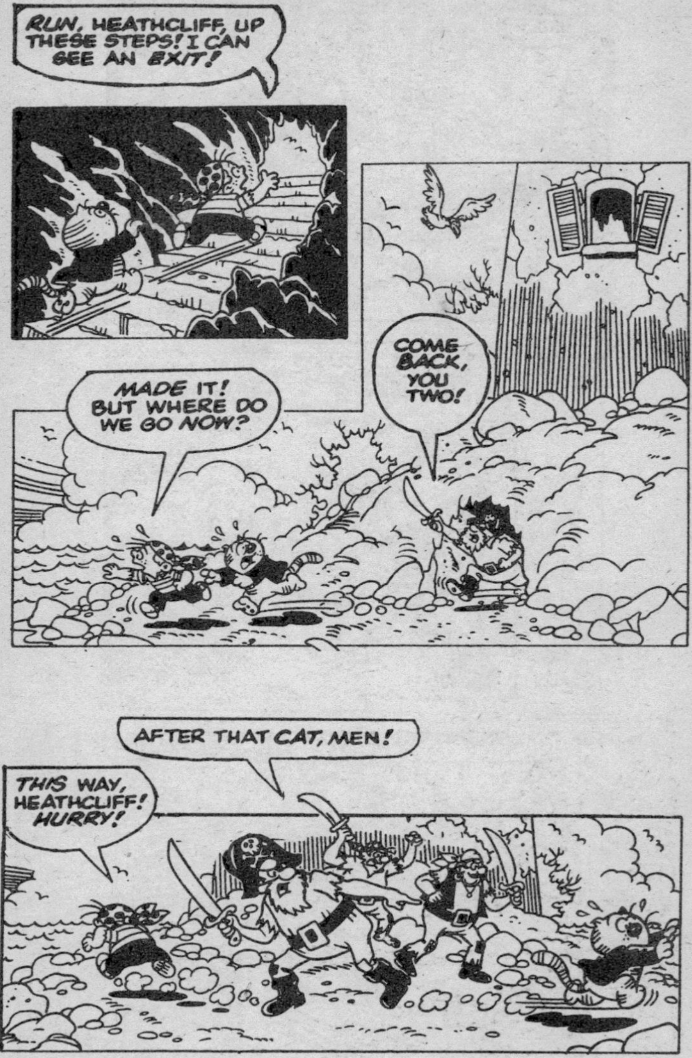
RUN, HEATHCLIFF, UP THESE STEPS! I CAN SEE AN EXIT!
MADE IT! BUT WHERE DO WE GO NOW?
COME BACK, YOU TWO!
AFTER THAT CAT, MEN!
THIS WAY, HEATHCLIFF! HURRY!

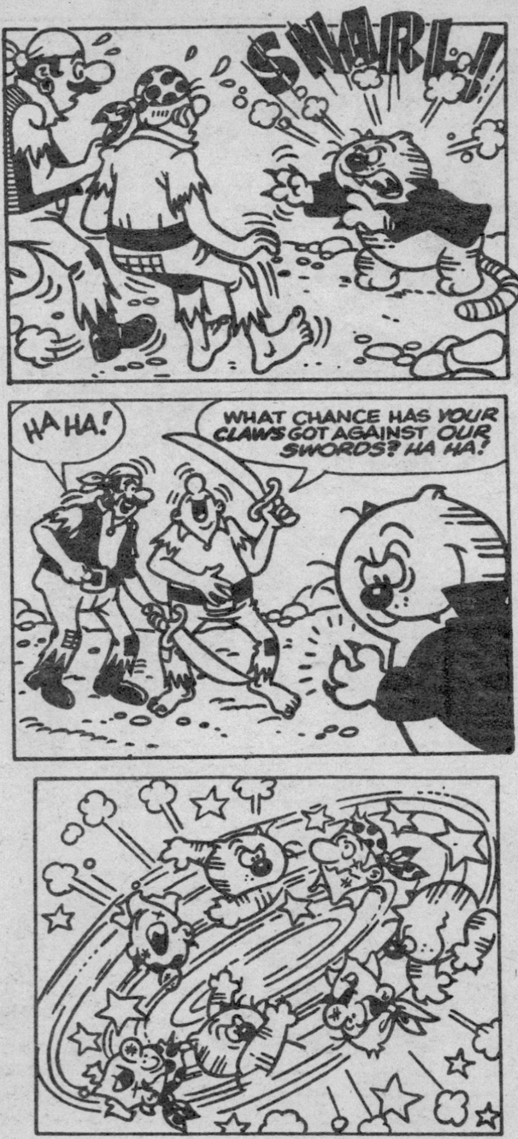

SNARL!
HA HA!
WHAT CHANCE HAS YOUR CLAWS GOT AGAINST OUR SWORDS? HA HA!

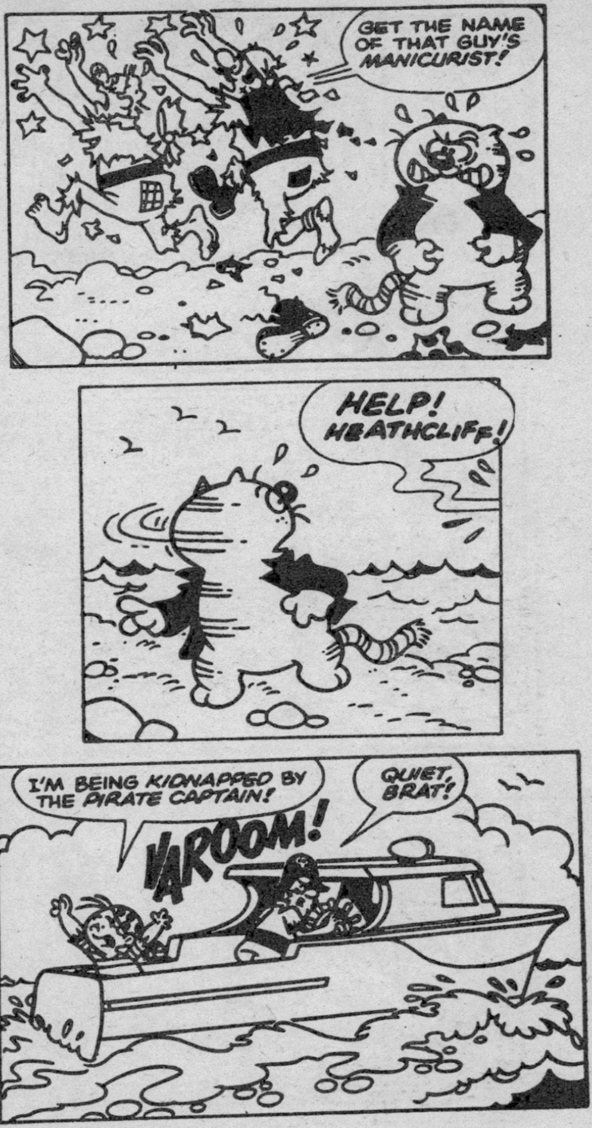
GET THE NAME OF THAT GUY'S MANICURIST!
HELP! HEATHCLIFF!
I'M BEING KIDNAPPED BY THE PIRATE CAPTAIN!
QUIET, BRAT!
VAROOM!

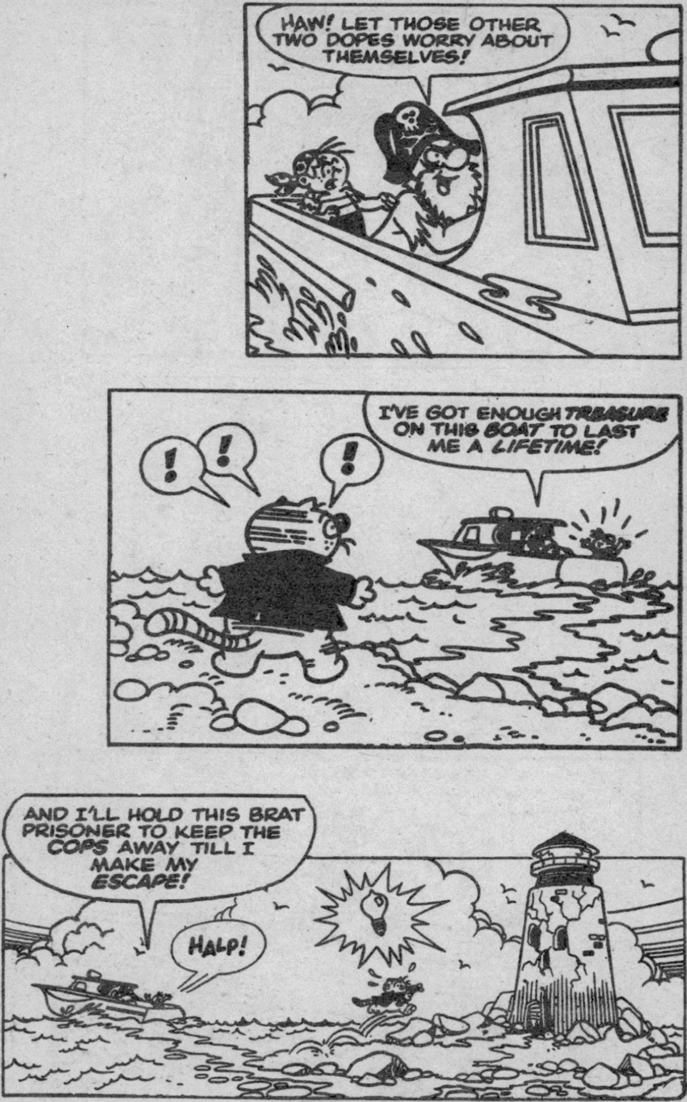
HAW! LET THOSE OTHER TWO DOPES WORRY ABOUT THEMSELVES!
!
!
!
I'VE GOT ENOUGH TREASURE ON THIS BOAT TO LAST ME A LIFETIME!
AND I'LL HOLD THIS BRAT PRISONER TO KEEP THE COPS AWAY TILL I MAKE MY ESCAPE!
HALP!

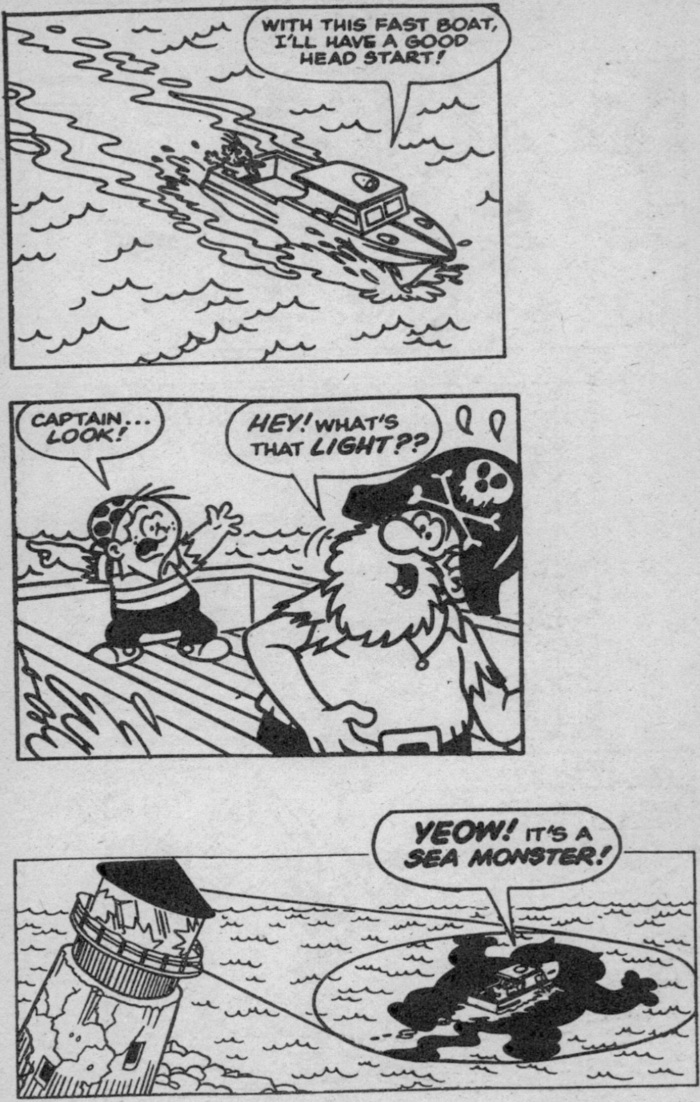
WITH THIS FAST BOAT, I'LL HAVE A GOOD HEAD START!
CAPTAIN... LOOK!
HEY! WHAT'S THAT LIGHT??
YEOW! IT'S A SEA MONSTER!

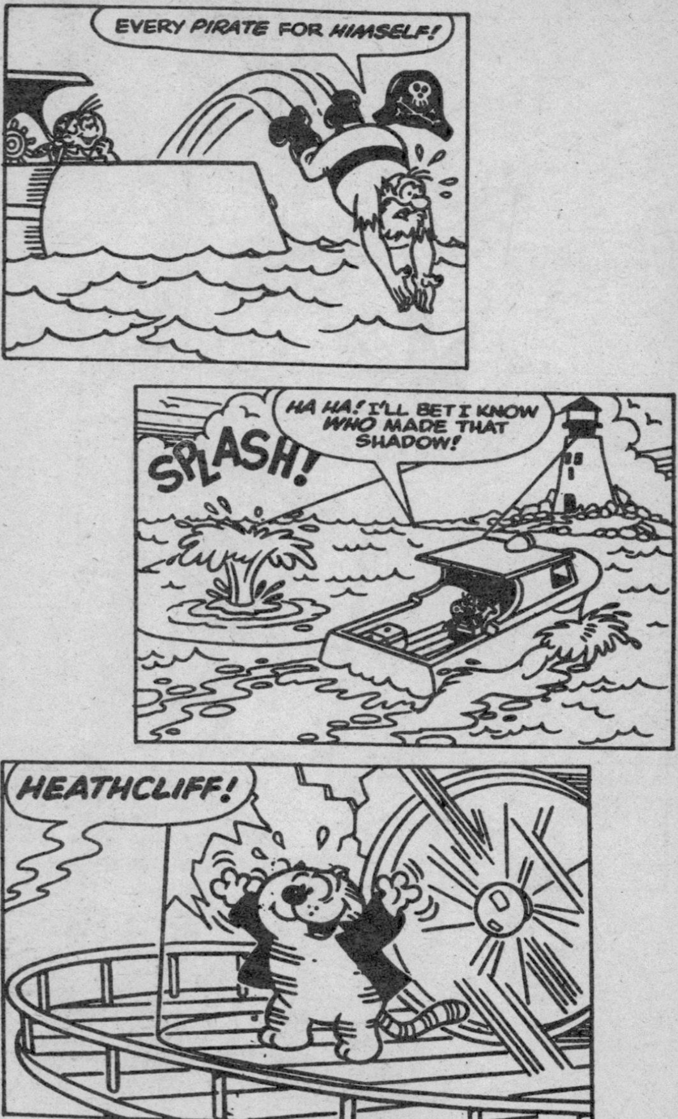
EVERY PIRATE FOR HIMSELF!
SPLASH!
HA HA! I'LL BET I KNOW WHO MADE THAT SHADOW!
HEATHCLIFF!

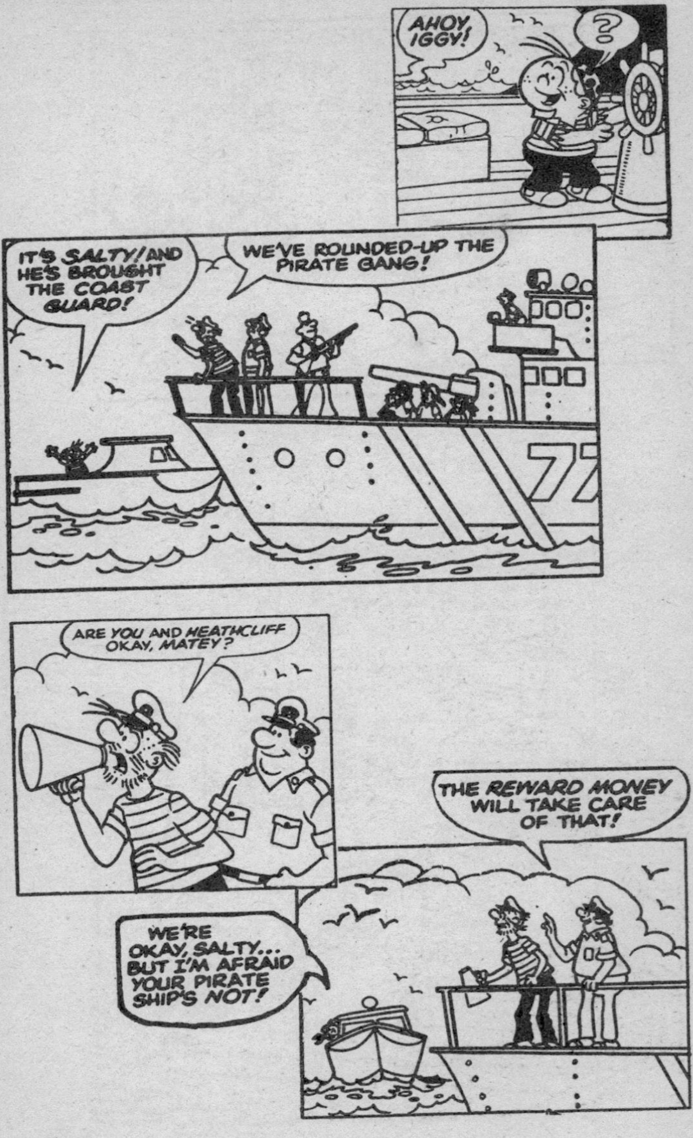
AHOY, IGGY!
?
IT'S SALTY! AND HE'S BROUGHT THE COAST GUARD!
WE'VE ROUNDED-UP THE PIRATE GANG!
ARE YOU AND HEATHCLIFF OKAY, MATEY?
WE'RE OKAY, SALTY... BUT I'M AFRAID YOUR PIRATE SHIP'S NOT!
THE REWARD MONEY WILL TAKE CARE OF THAT!

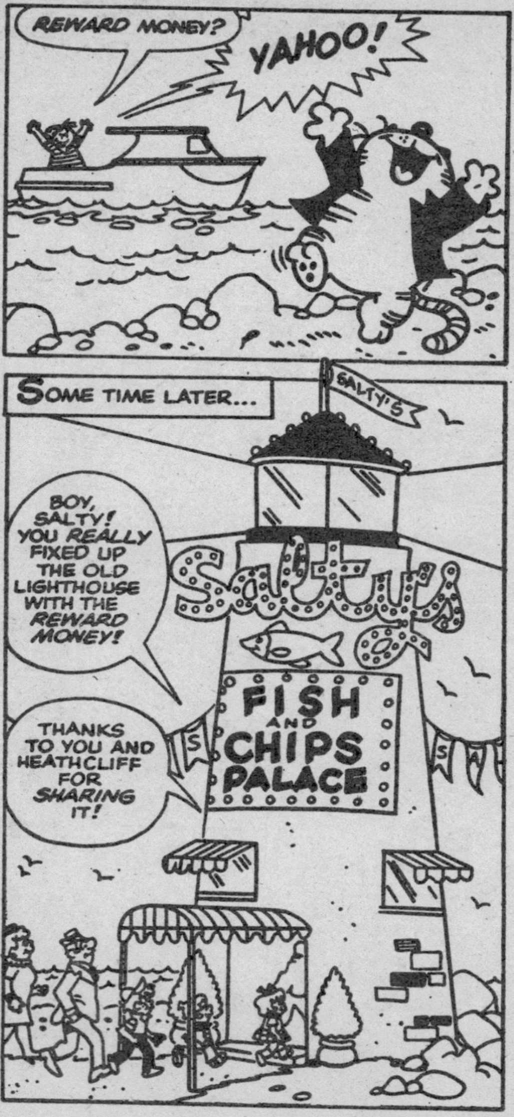
REWARD MONEY?
YAHOO!
SOME TIME LATER...
SALTY'S
Salty's
FISH AND CHIPS PALACE
BOY, SALTY! YOU REALLY FIXED UP THE OLD LIGHTHOUSE WITH THE REWARD MONEY!
THANKS TO YOU AND HEATHCLIFF FOR SHARING IT!

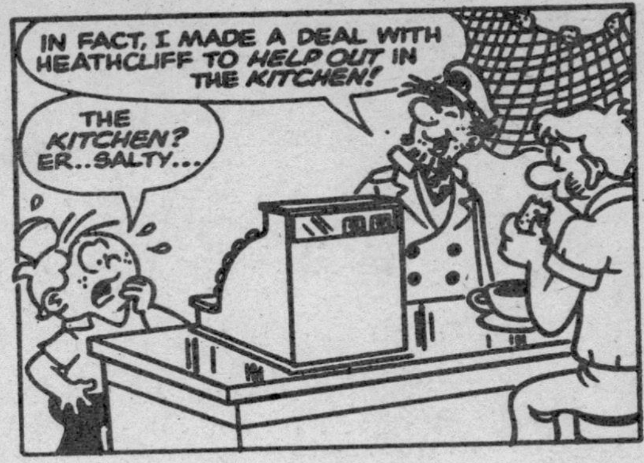
IN FACT, I MADE A DEAL WITH HEATHCLIFF TO HELP OUT IN THE KITCHEN!
THE KITCHEN? ER...SALTY...

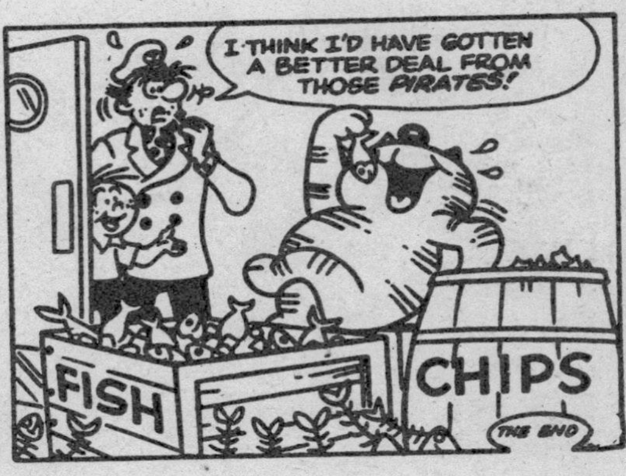
I THINK I'D HAVE GOTTEN A BETTER DEAL FROM THOSE PIRATES!
FISH
CHIPS
THE END

HEATHCLIFF in FRIGHT DAY AT THE BIJOU

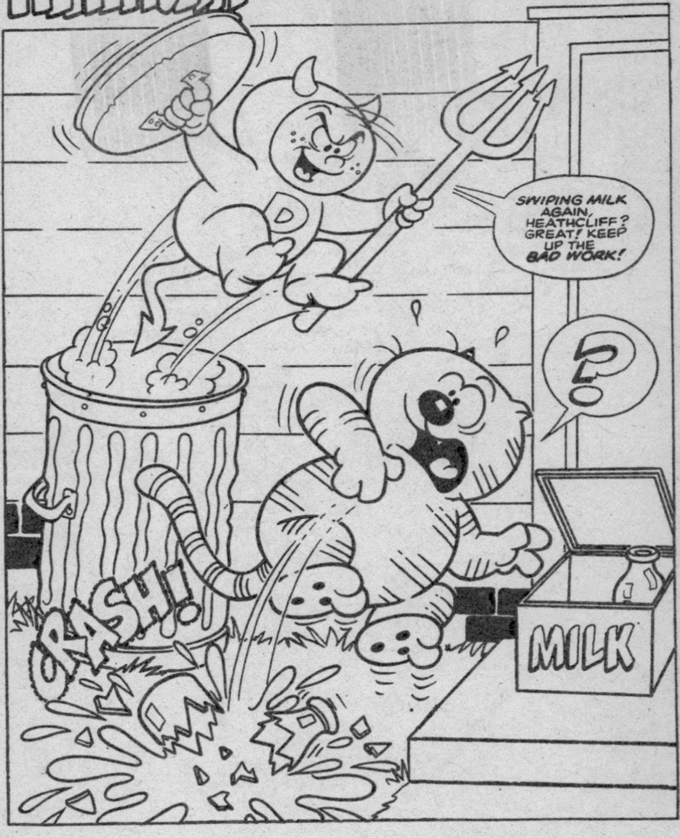
SWIPING MILK AGAIN, HEATHCLIFF? GREAT! KEEP UP THE BAD WORK!
?
CRASH!
MILK

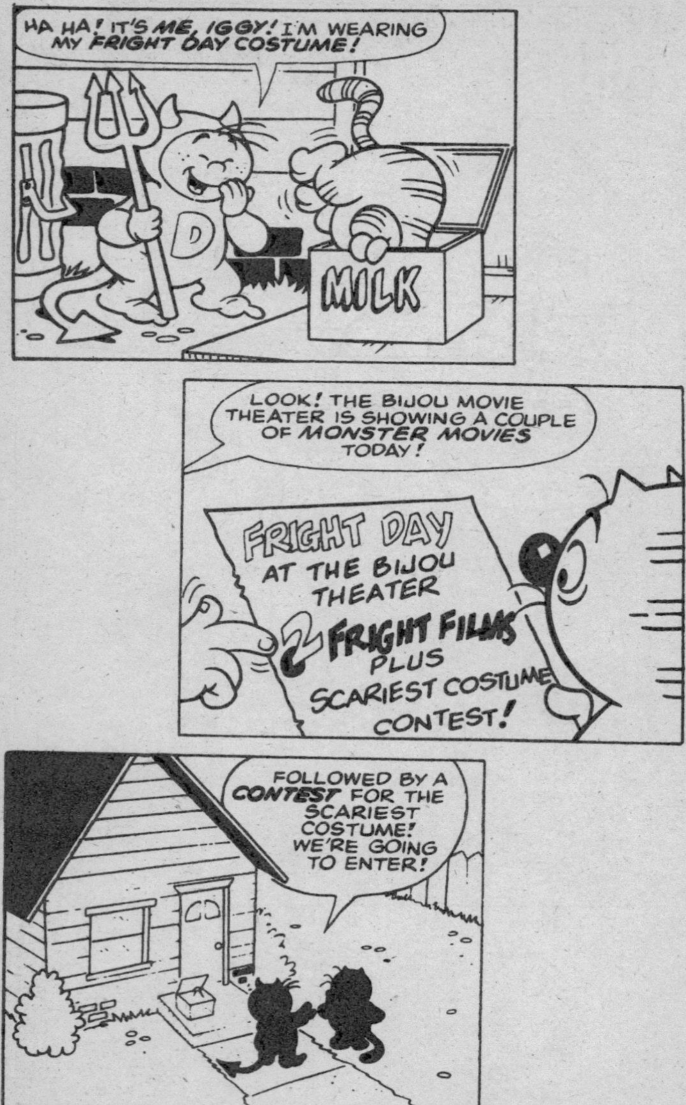
HA HA! IT'S ME, IGGY! I'M WEARING MY FRIGHT DAY COSTUME!
MILK
LOOK! THE BIJOU MOVIE THEATER IS SHOWING A COUPLE OF MONSTER MOVIES TODAY!
FRIGHT DAY AT THE BIJOU THEATER 2 FRIGHT FILMS PLUS SCARIEST COSTUME CONTEST!
FOLLOWED BY A CONTEST FOR THE SCARIEST COSTUME! WE'RE GOING TO ENTER!

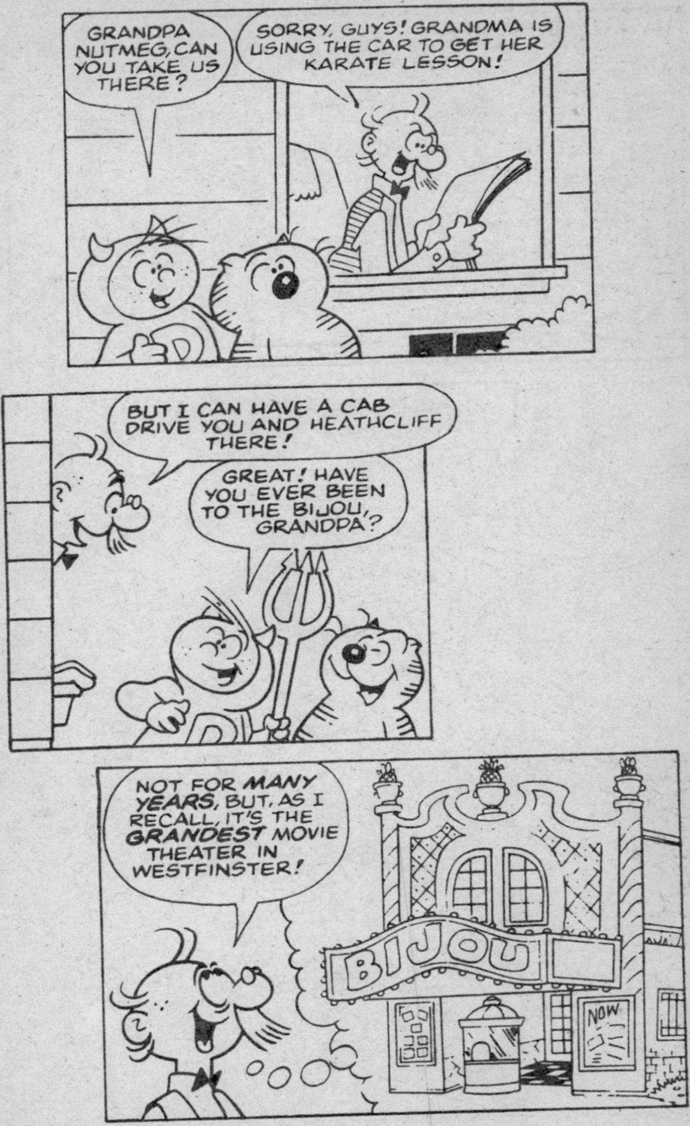
GRANDPA NUTMEG, CAN YOU TAKE US THERE?
SORRY, GUYS! GRANDMA IS USING THE CAR TO GET HER KARATE LESSON!
BUT I CAN HAVE A CAB DRIVE YOU AND HEATHCLIFF THERE!
GREAT! HAVE YOU EVER BEEN TO THE BIJOU, GRANDPA?
NOT FOR MANY YEARS, BUT, AS I RECALL, IT'S THE GRANDEST MOVIE THEATER IN WESTFINSTER!
BIJOU
NOW

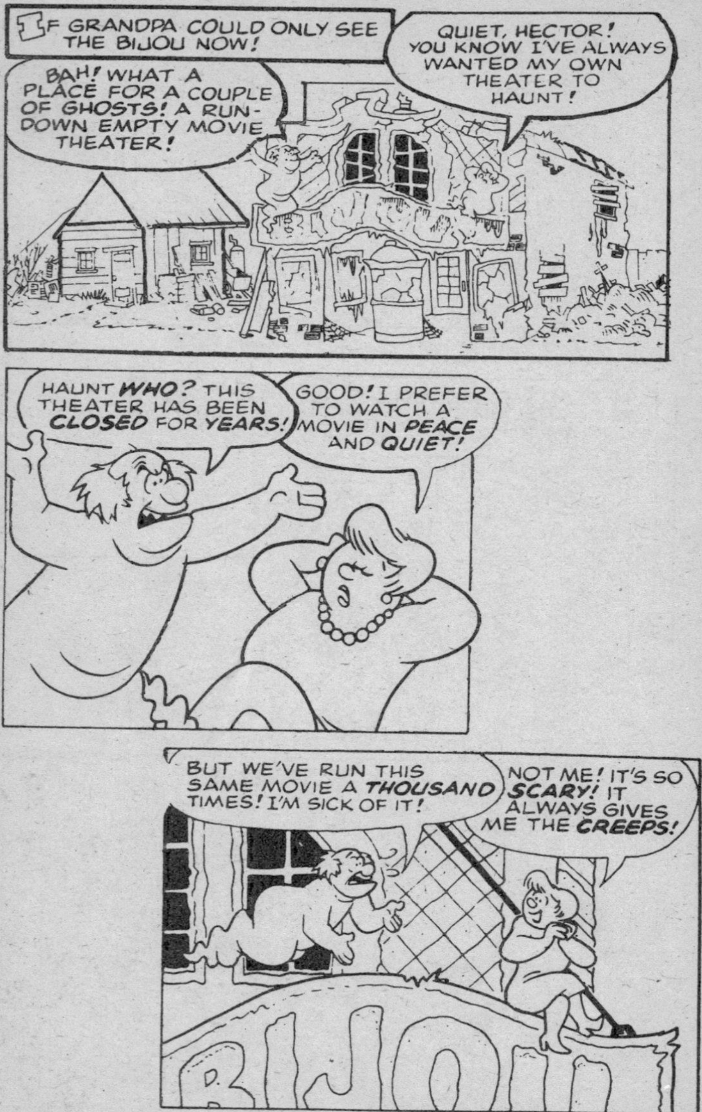
IF GRANDPA COULD ONLY SEE THE BIJOU NOW!
QUIET, HECTOR! YOU KNOW I'VE ALWAYS WANTED MY OWN THEATER TO HAUNT!
BAH! WHAT A PLACE FOR A COUPLE OF GHOSTS! A RUN-DOWN EMPTY MOVIE THEATER!
HAUNT WHO? THIS THEATER HAS BEEN CLOSED FOR YEARS!
GOOD! I PREFER TO WATCH A MOVIE IN PEACE AND QUIET!
BUT WE'VE RUN THIS SAME MOVIE A THOUSAND TIMES! I'M SICK OF IT!
NOT ME! IT'S SO SCARY! IT ALWAYS GIVES ME THE CREEPS!
BIJOU

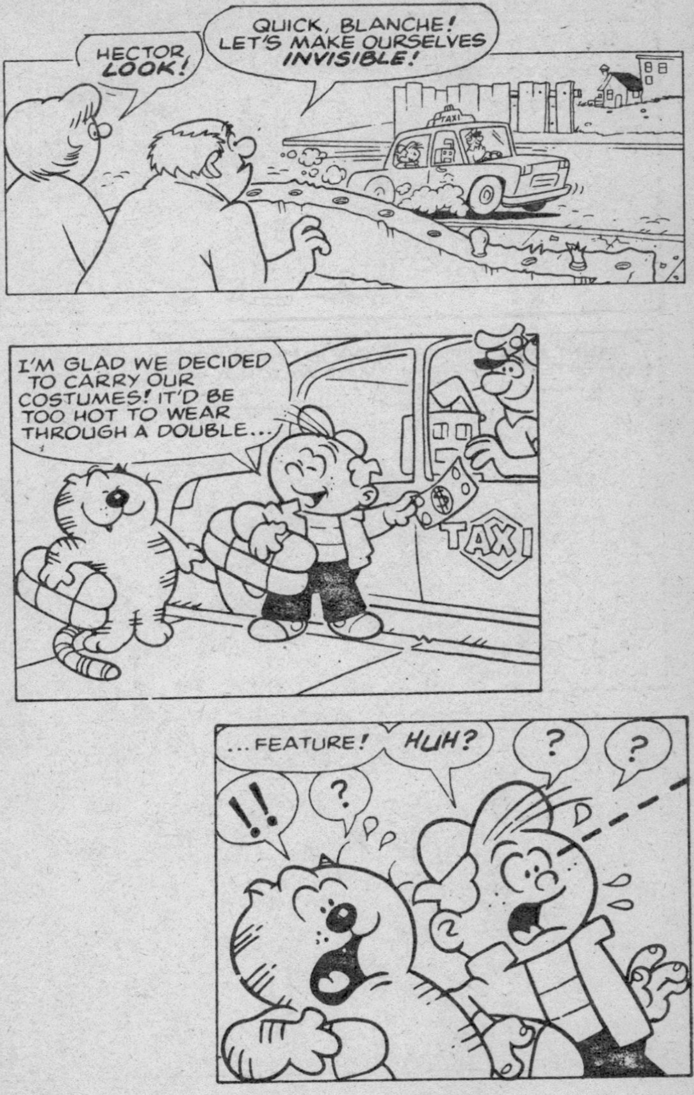
HECTOR, LOOK!
QUICK, BLANCHE! LET'S MAKE OURSELVES INVISIBLE!
TAXI
I'M GLAD WE DECIDED TO CARRY OUR COSTUMES! IT'D BE TOO HOT TO WEAR THROUGH A DOUBLE...
TAXI
...FEATURE!
HUH?
?
?
!!
?

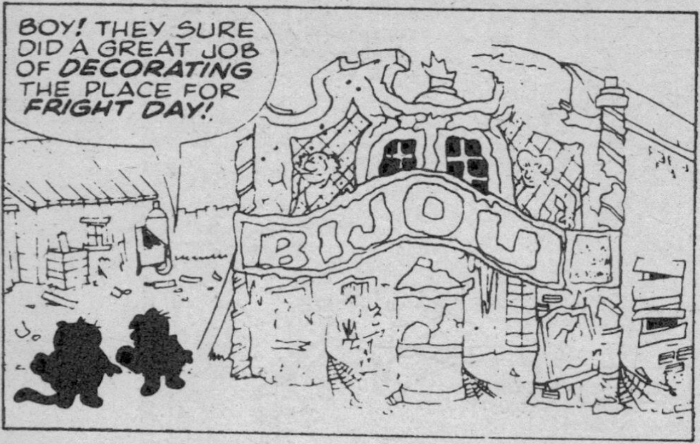
BOY! THEY SURE DID A GREAT JOB OF DECORATING THE PLACE FOR FRIGHT DAY!
BIJOU

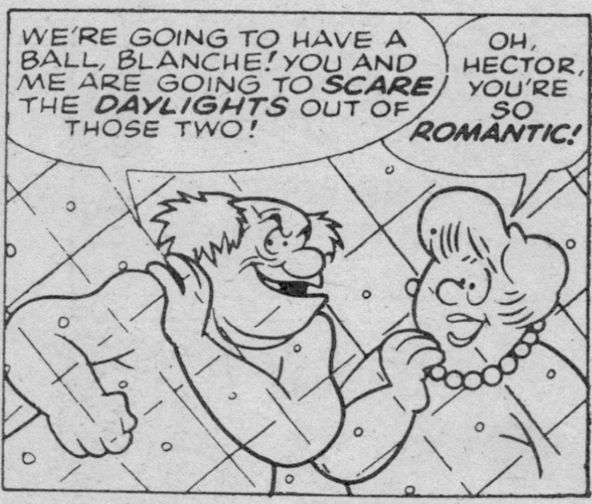
WE'RE GOING TO HAVE A BALL, BLANCHE! YOU AND ME ARE GOING TO SCARE THE DAYLIGHTS OUT OF THOSE TWO!
OH, HECTOR, YOU'RE SO ROMANTIC!

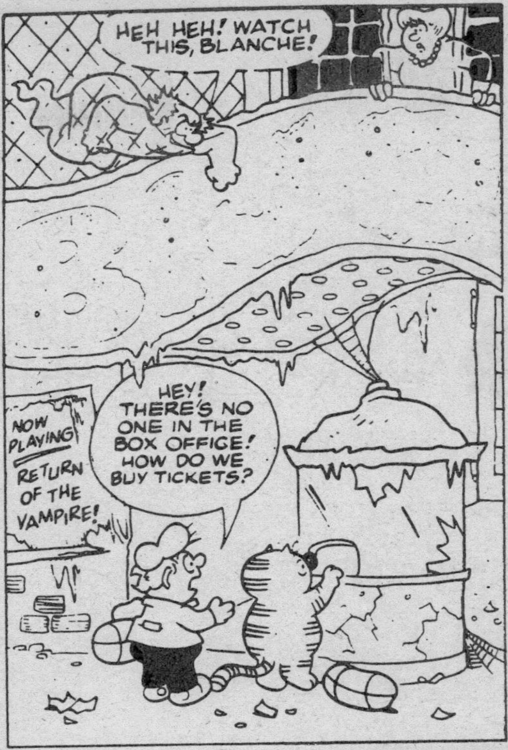
HEH HEH! WATCH THIS, BLANCHE!
NOW PLAYING
RETURN OF THE VAMPIRE!
HEY! THERE'S NO ONE IN THE BOX OFFICE! HOW DO WE BUY TICKETS?

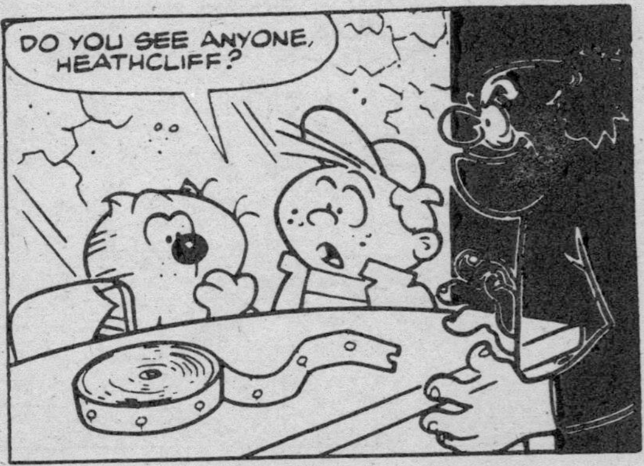
DO YOU SEE ANYONE, HEATHCLIFF?

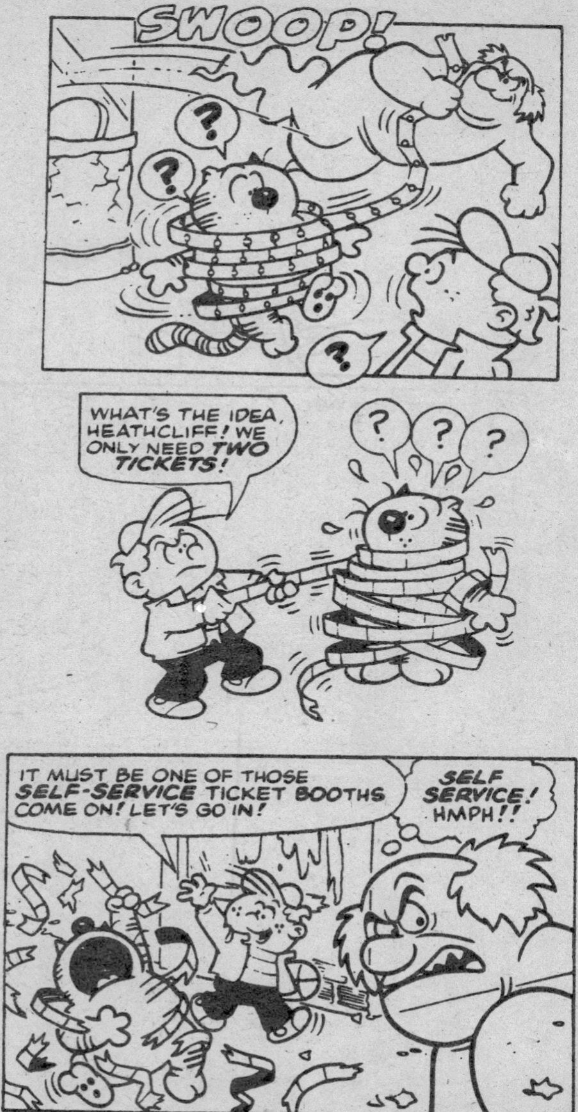
SWOOP!
?
?
?
WHAT'S THE IDEA, HEATHCLIFF! WE ONLY NEED TWO TICKETS!
?
?
?
IT MUST BE ONE OF THOSE SELF-SERVICE TICKET BOOTHS COME ON! LET'S GO IN!
SELF SERVICE! HMPH!!

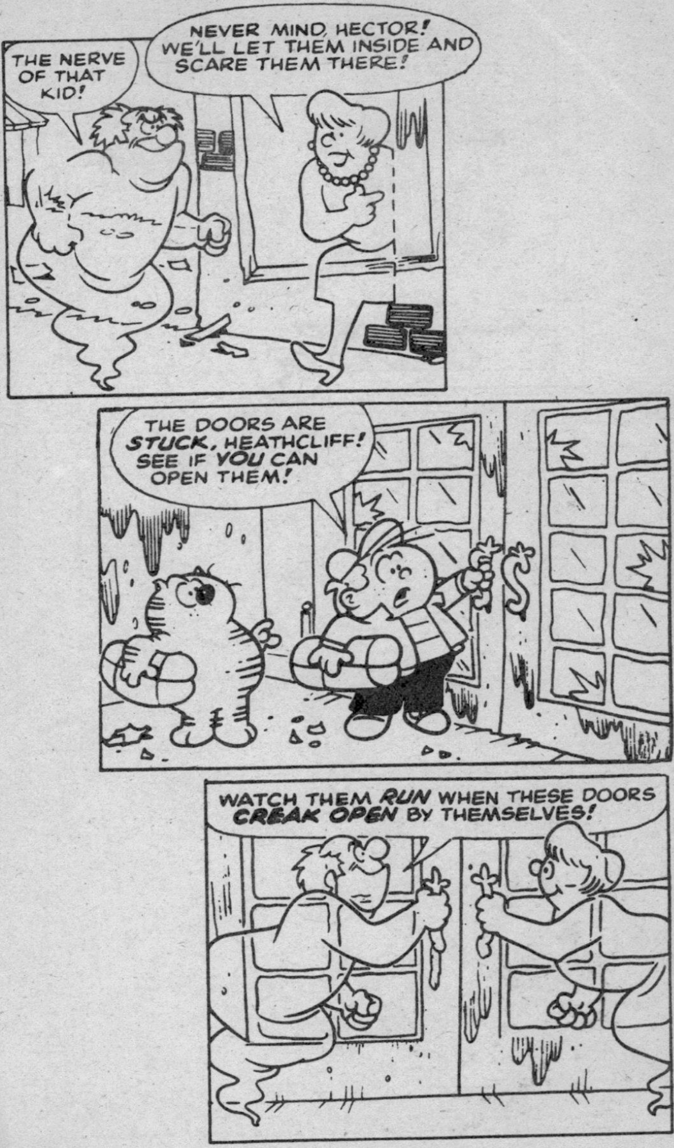
THE NERVE OF THAT KID!
NEVER MIND, HECTOR! WE'LL LET THEM INSIDE AND SCARE THEM THERE!
THE DOORS ARE STUCK, HEATHCLIFF! SEE IF YOU CAN OPEN THEM!
WATCH THEM RUN WHEN THESE DOORS CREAK OPEN BY THEMSELVES!

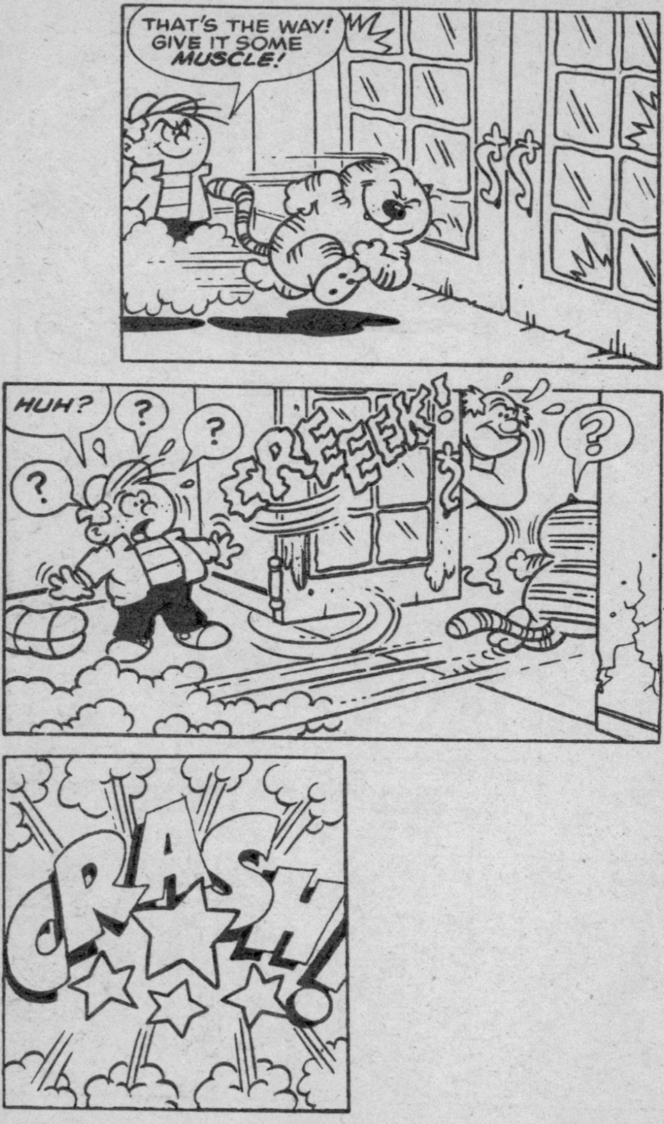
THAT'S THE WAY! GIVE IT SOME *MUSCLE!*
HUH?
?
?
?
CREEEK!
?
CRASH!

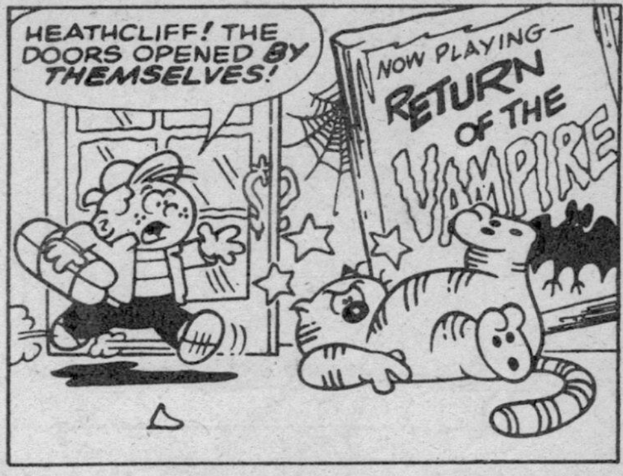
HEATHCLIFF! THE DOORS OPENED BY THEMSELVES!
NOW PLAYING—
RETURN OF THE VAMPIRE

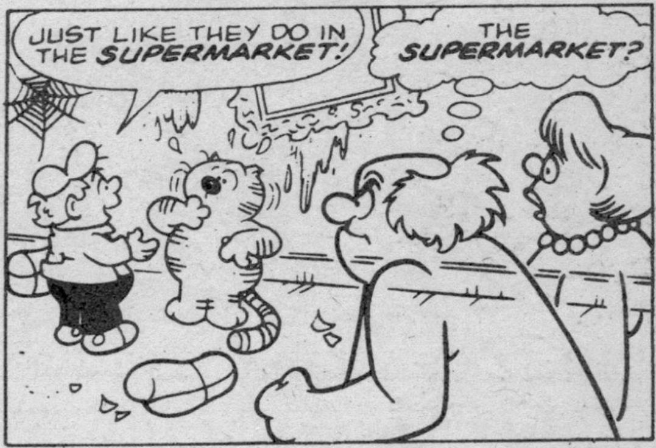
JUST LIKE THEY DO IN THE SUPERMARKET!
THE SUPERMARKET?

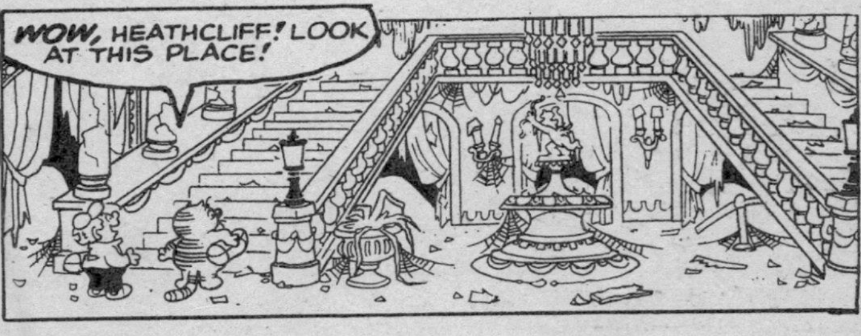
WOW, HEATHCLIFF! LOOK AT THIS PLACE!

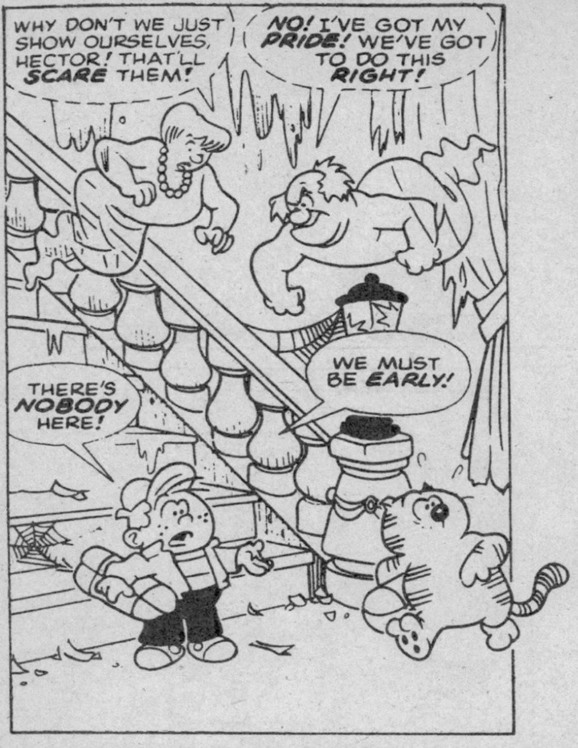
WHY DON'T WE JUST SHOW OURSELVES, HECTOR! THAT'LL SCARE THEM!
NO! I'VE GOT MY PRIDE! WE'VE GOT TO DO THIS RIGHT!
THERE'S NOBODY HERE!
WE MUST BE EARLY!

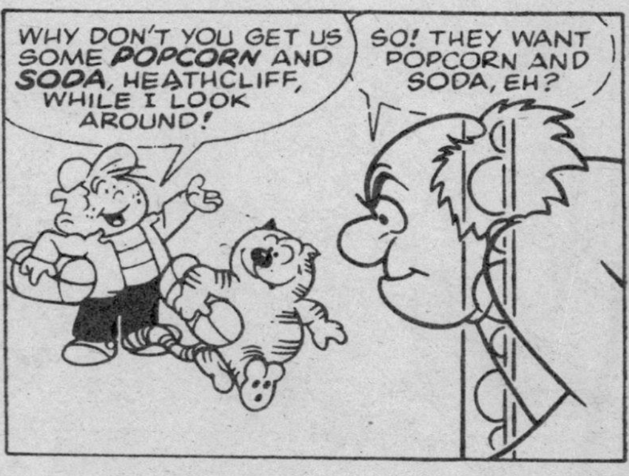
WHY DON'T YOU GET US SOME POPCORN AND SODA, HEATHCLIFF, WHILE I LOOK AROUND!
SO! THEY WANT POPCORN AND SODA, EH?

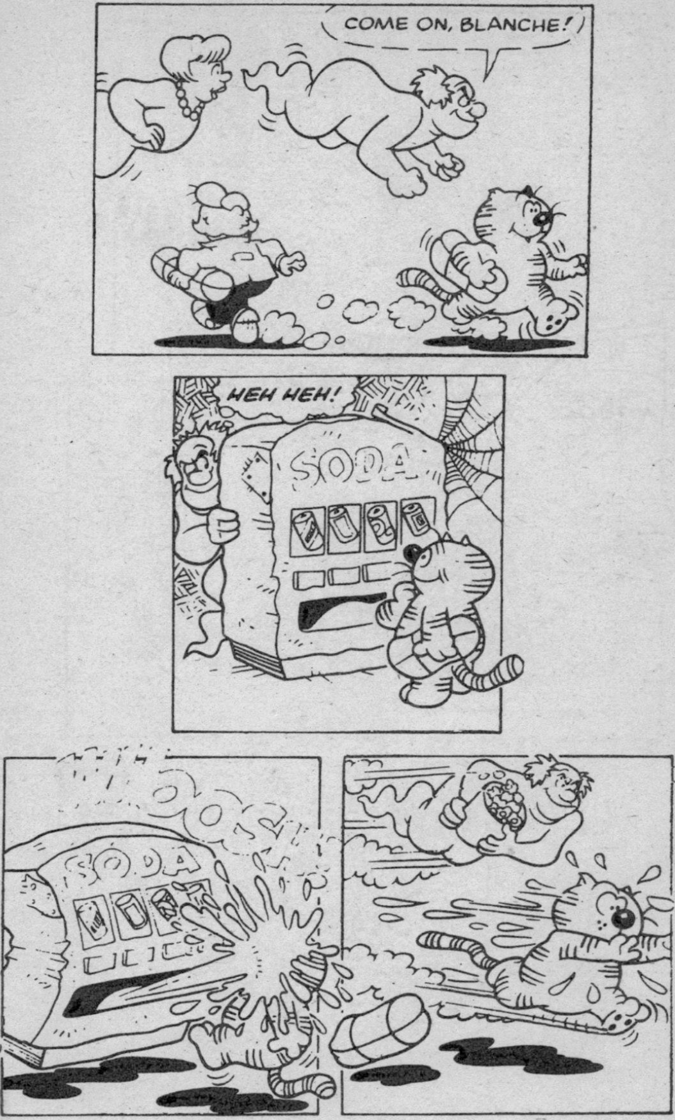
COME ON, BLANCHE!
HEH HEH!

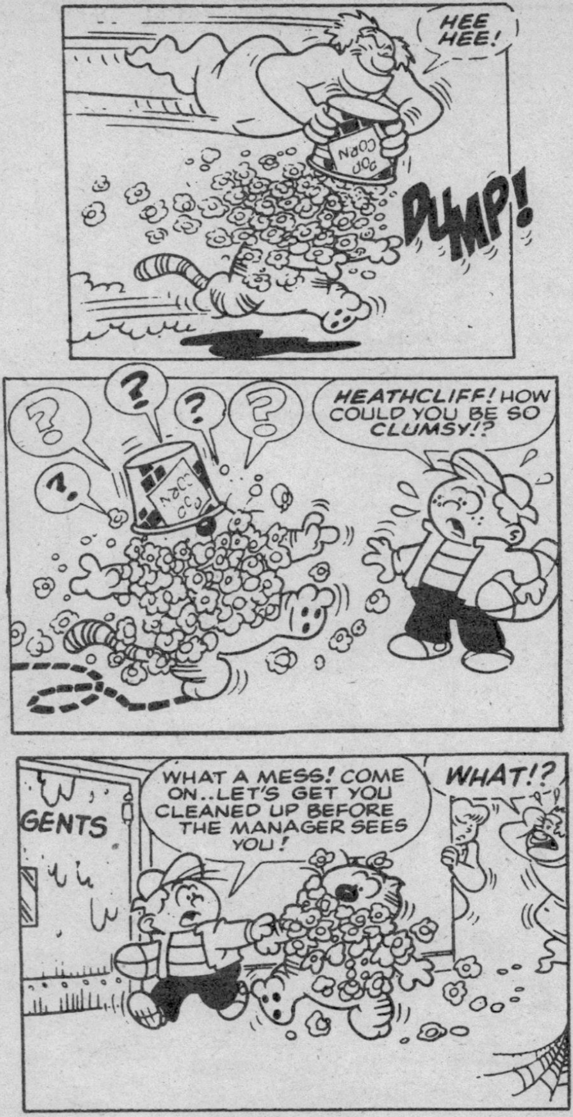
HEE HEE!
POP CORN
DUMP!
?
?
?
?
?
HEATHCLIFF! HOW COULD YOU BE SO CLUMSY!?
GENTS
WHAT A MESS! COME ON..LET'S GET YOU CLEANED UP BEFORE THE MANAGER SEES YOU!
WHAT!?

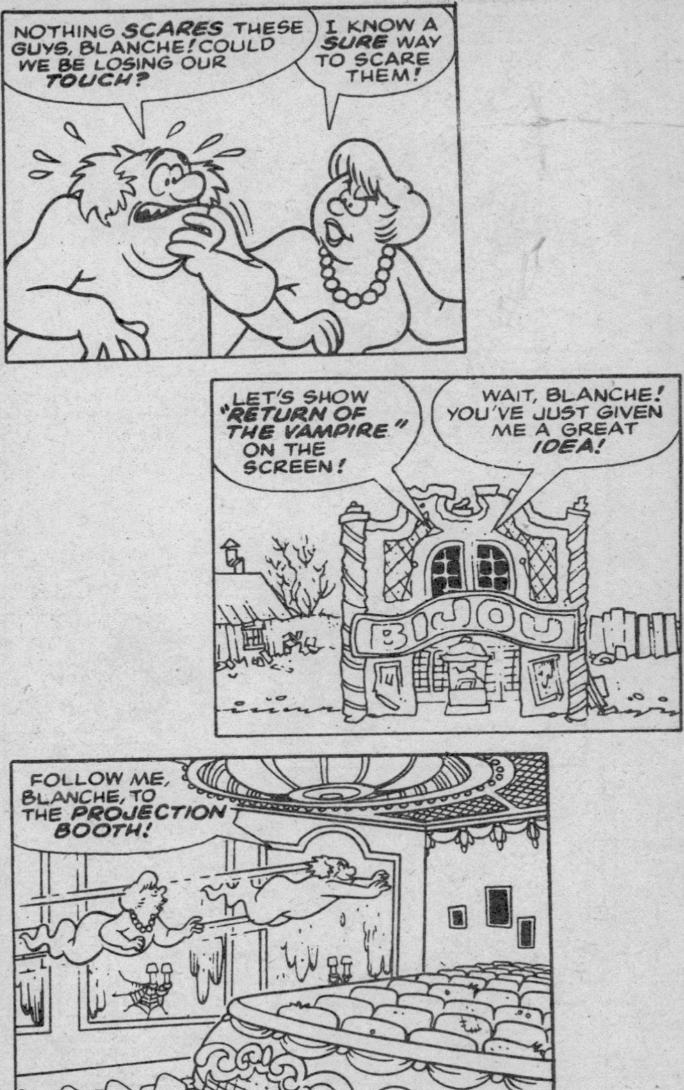
NOTHING SCARES THESE GUYS, BLANCHE! COULD WE BE LOSING OUR TOUCH?
I KNOW A SURE WAY TO SCARE THEM!
LET'S SHOW "RETURN OF THE VAMPIRE" ON THE SCREEN!
WAIT, BLANCHE! YOU'VE JUST GIVEN ME A GREAT IDEA!
BIJOU
FOLLOW ME, BLANCHE, TO THE PROJECTION BOOTH!

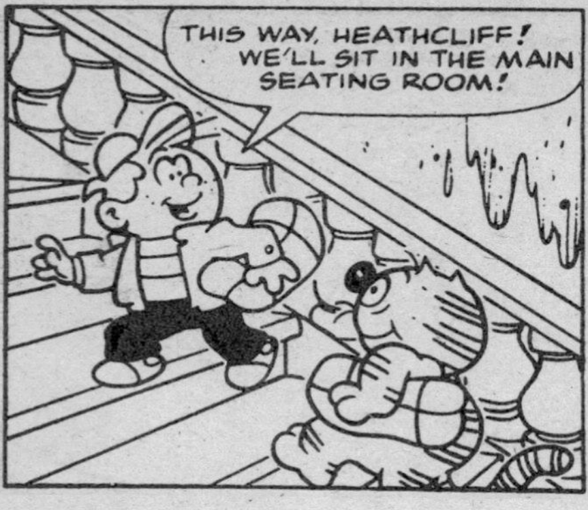
THIS WAY, HEATHCLIFF! WE'LL SIT IN THE MAIN SEATING ROOM!

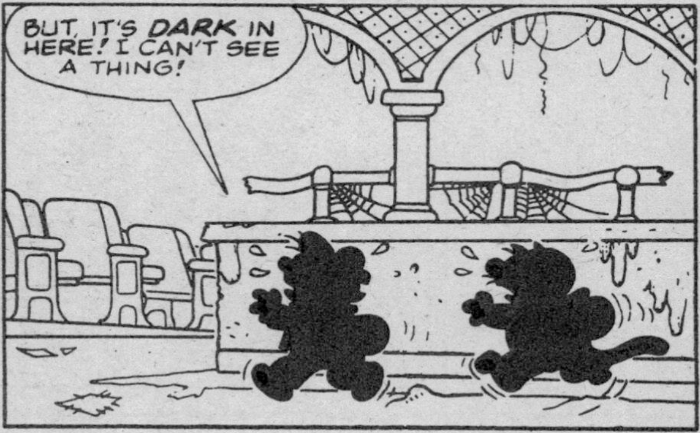
BUT, IT'S DARK IN HERE! I CAN'T SEE A THING!

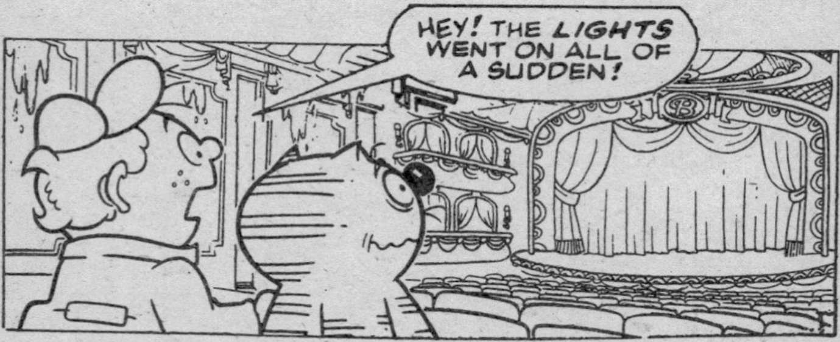
HEY! THE LIGHTS WENT ON ALL OF A SUDDEN!

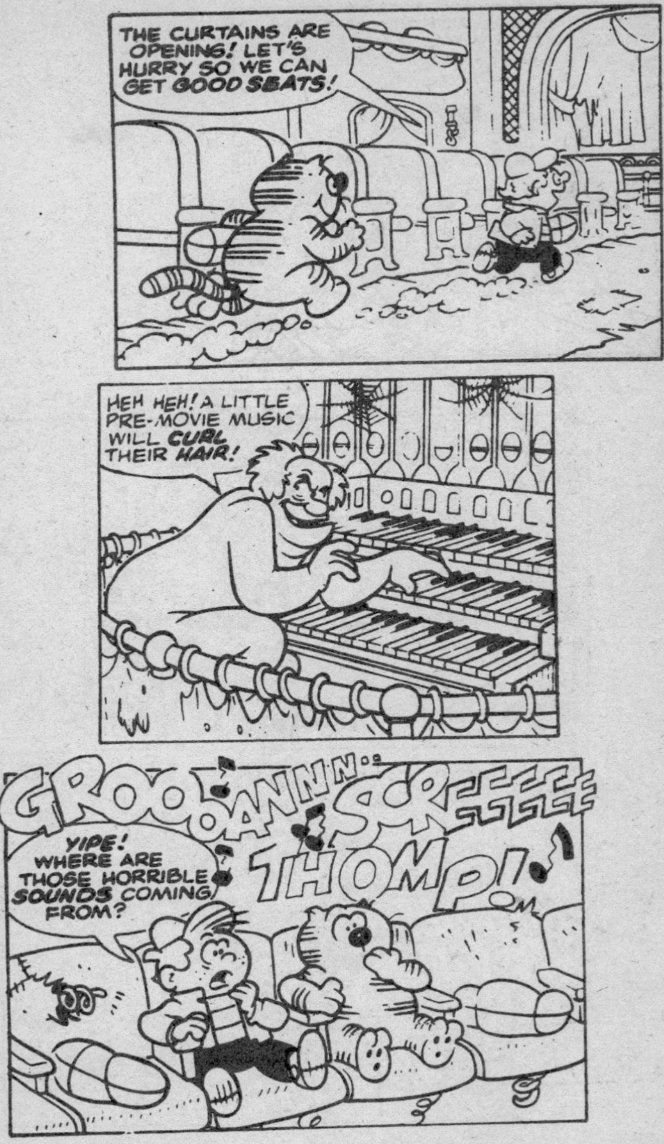
THE CURTAINS ARE OPENING! LET'S HURRY SO WE CAN GET GOOD SEATS!
HEH HEH! A LITTLE PRE-MOVIE MUSIC WILL CURL THEIR HAIR!
GROOOANNN SCREEEEE
THOMP!
YIPE! WHERE ARE THOSE HORRIBLE SOUNDS COMING FROM?

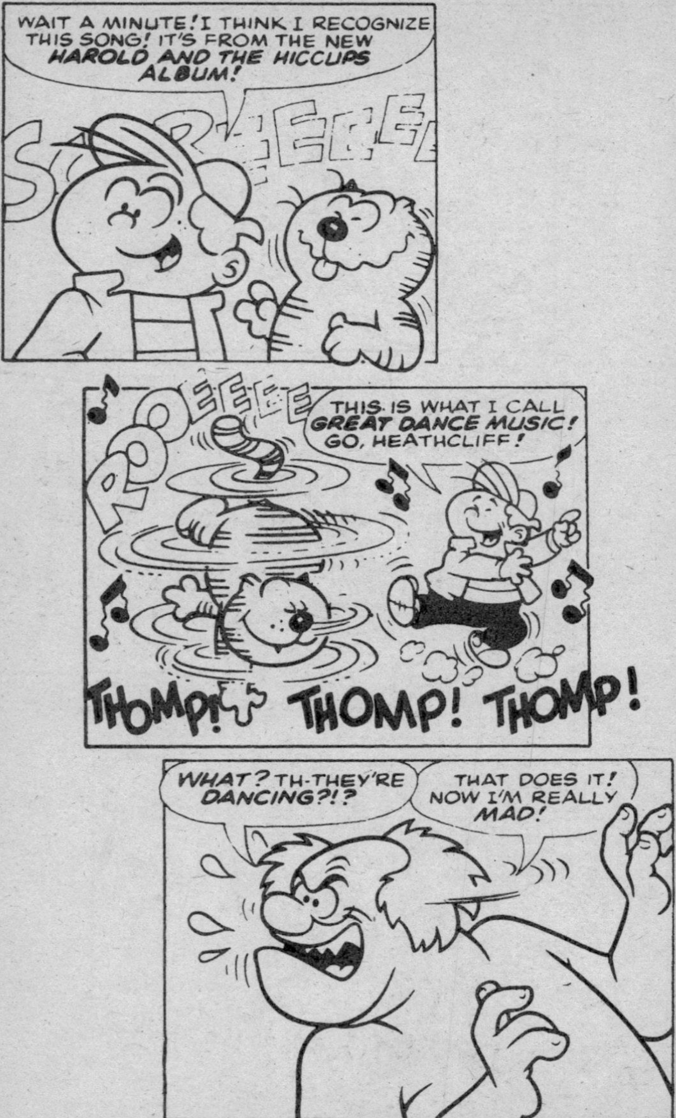
WAIT A MINUTE! I THINK I RECOGNIZE THIS SONG! IT'S FROM THE NEW HAROLD AND THE HICCUPS ALBUM!
SPREEEEE
ROOEEEEE
THIS IS WHAT I CALL GREAT DANCE MUSIC! GO, HEATHCLIFF!
THOMP! THOMP! THOMP!
WHAT? TH-THEY'RE DANCING?!?
THAT DOES IT! NOW I'M REALLY MAD!

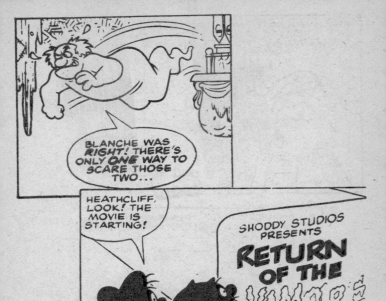

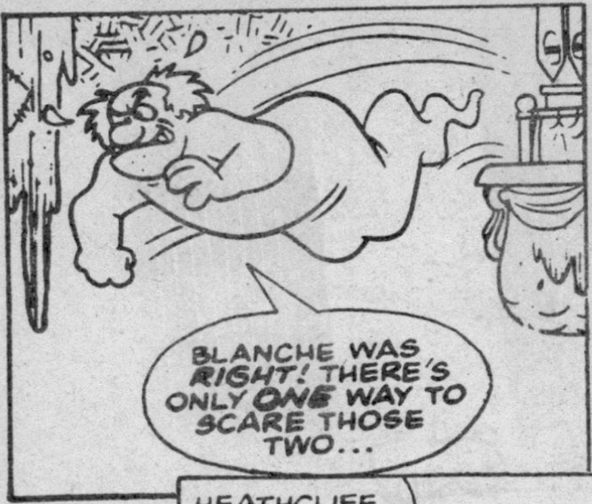
BLANCHE WAS RIGHT! THERE'S ONLY ONE WAY TO SCARE THOSE TWO...

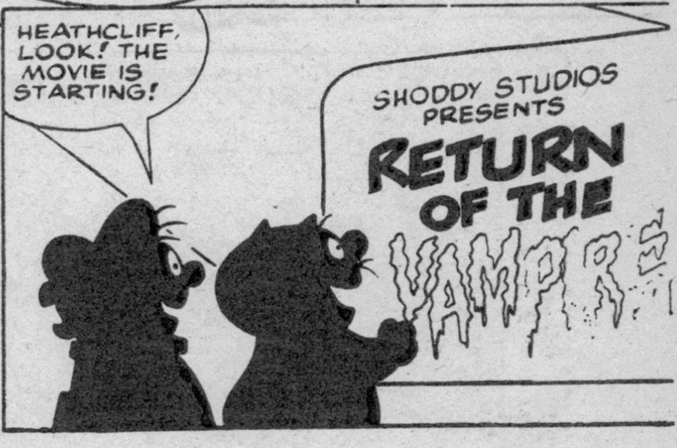
HEATHCLIFF, LOOK! THE MOVIE IS STARTING!
SHODDY STUDIOS PRESENTS
RETURN OF THE

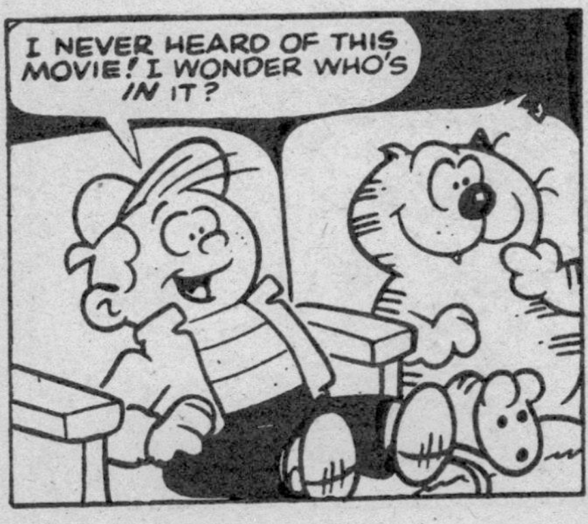
I NEVER HEARD OF THIS MOVIE! I WONDER WHO'S IN IT?

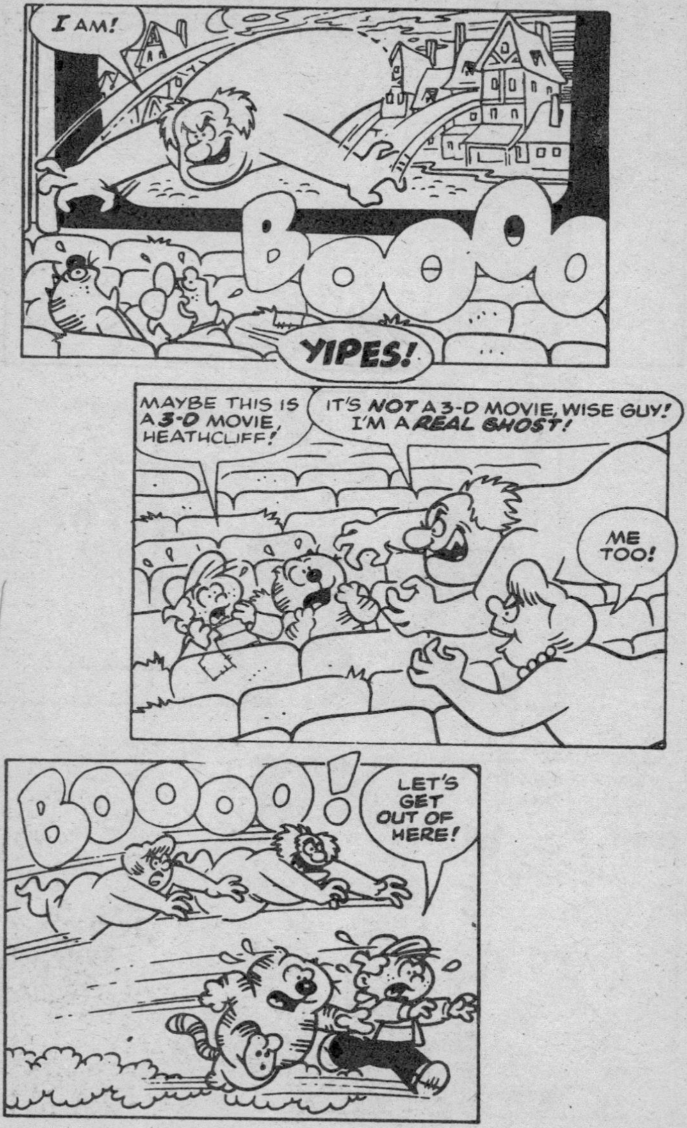
I AM!
BOOOO
YIPES!
MAYBE THIS IS A 3-D MOVIE, HEATHCLIFF!
IT'S NOT A 3-D MOVIE, WISE GUY! I'M A REAL GHOST!
ME TOO!
BOOOO!
LET'S GET OUT OF HERE!

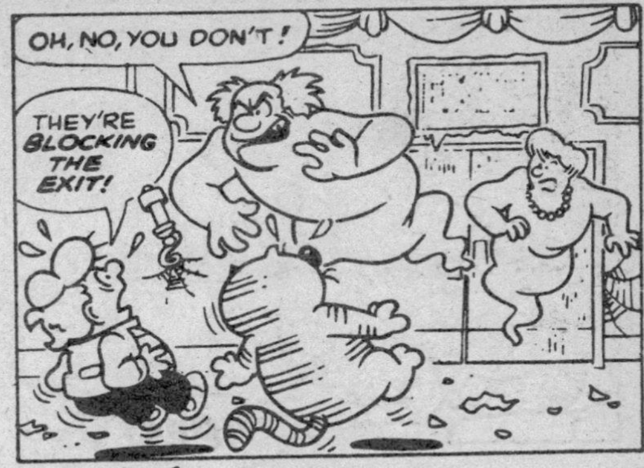
OH, NO, YOU DON'T!
THEY'RE BLOCKING THE EXIT!

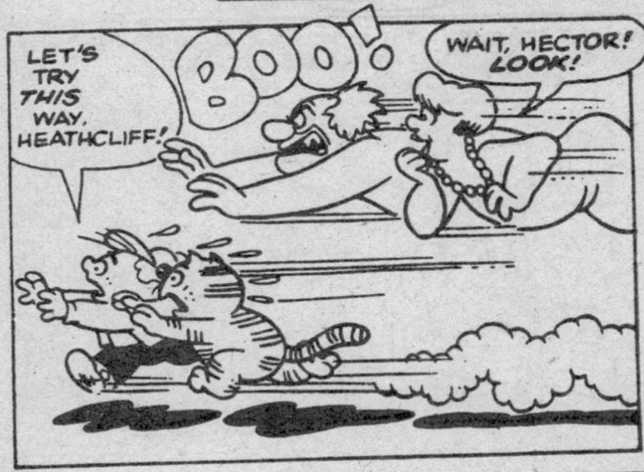
LET'S TRY THIS WAY, HEATHCLIFF!
BOO!
WAIT, HECTOR! LOOK!

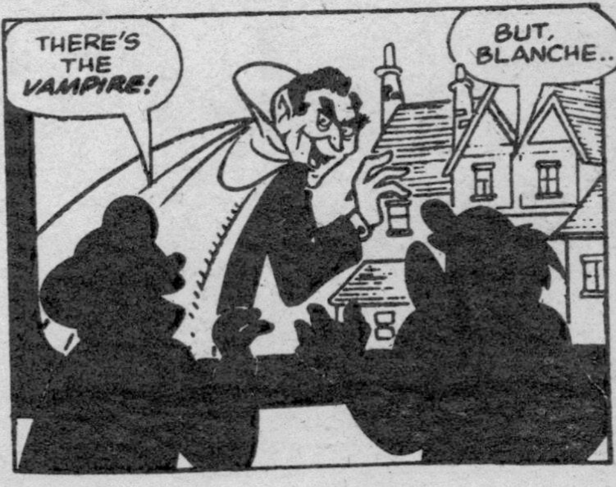
THERE'S THE VAMPIRE!
BUT, BLANCHE..

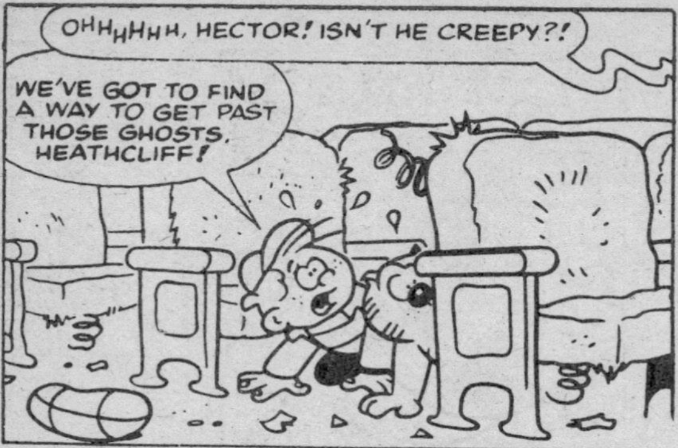
OHHHHHH, HECTOR! ISN'T HE CREEPY?!
WE'VE GOT TO FIND A WAY TO GET PAST THOSE GHOSTS, HEATHCLIFF!

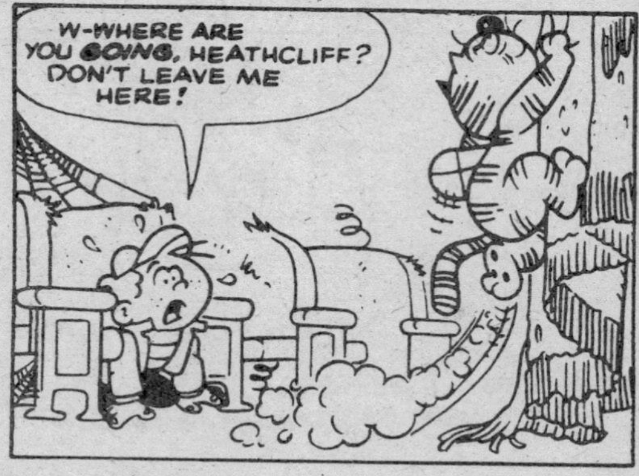
W-WHERE ARE YOU GOING, HEATHCLIFF? DON'T LEAVE ME HERE!

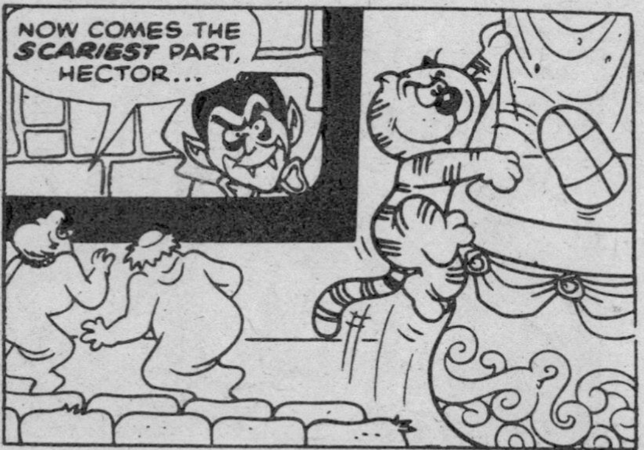
NOW COMES THE SCARIEST PART, HECTOR...

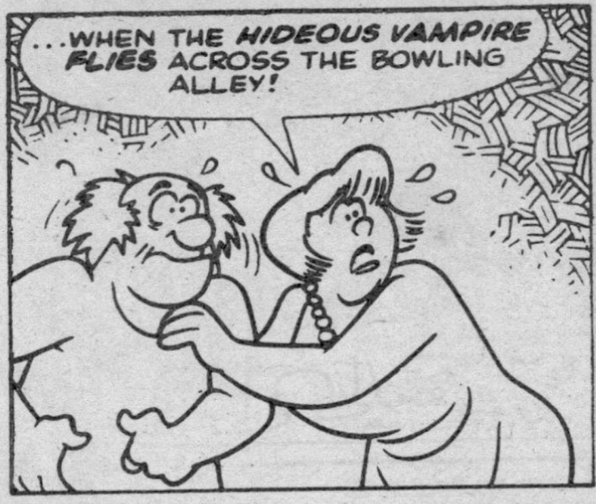
...WHEN THE HIDEOUS VAMPIRE FLIES ACROSS THE BOWLING ALLEY!

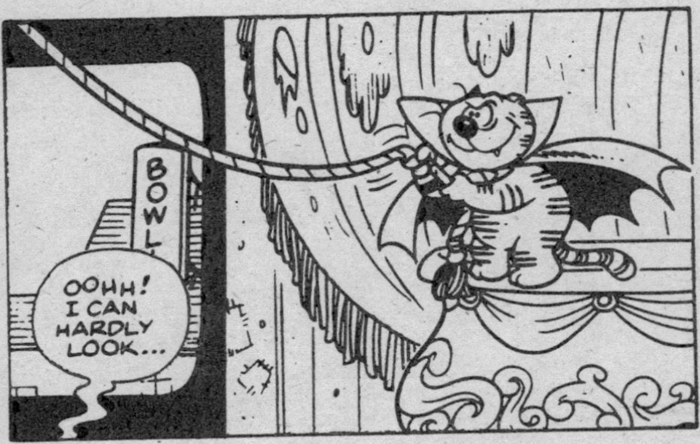
BOWL
OOHH! I CAN HARDLY LOOK...

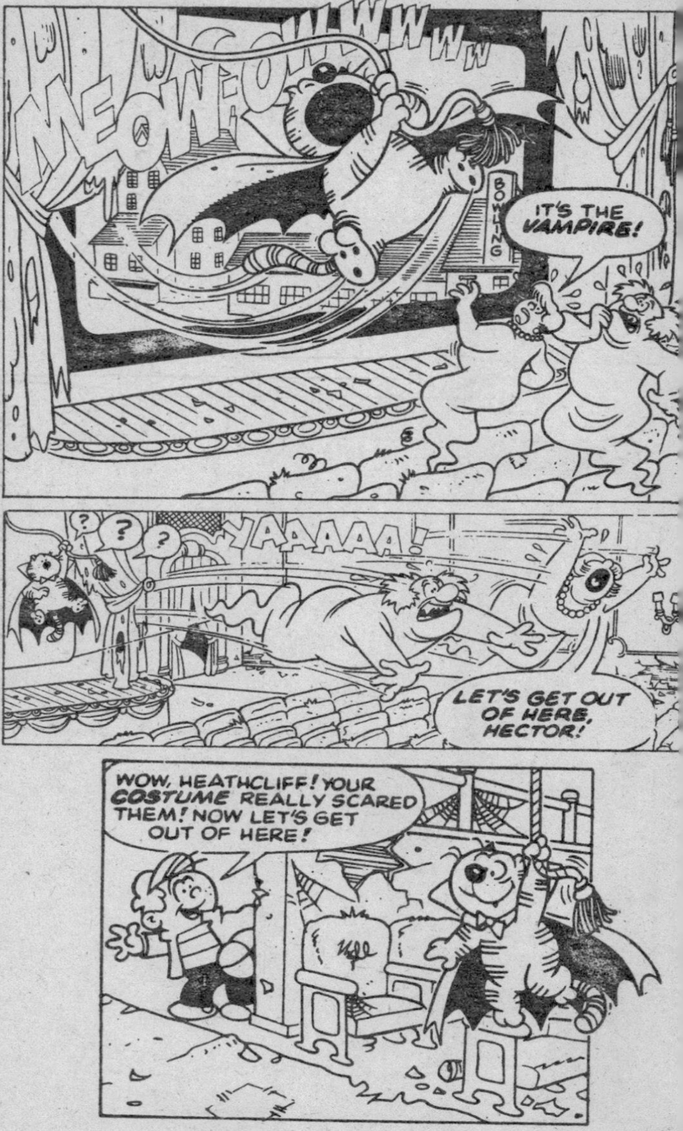
MEOWEOWWWWWW
BOWLING
IT'S THE VAMPIRE!
? ? ?
YAAAAA!
LET'S GET OUT OF HERE, HECTOR!
WOW, HEATHCLIFF! YOUR COSTUME REALLY SCARED THEM! NOW LET'S GET OUT OF HERE!

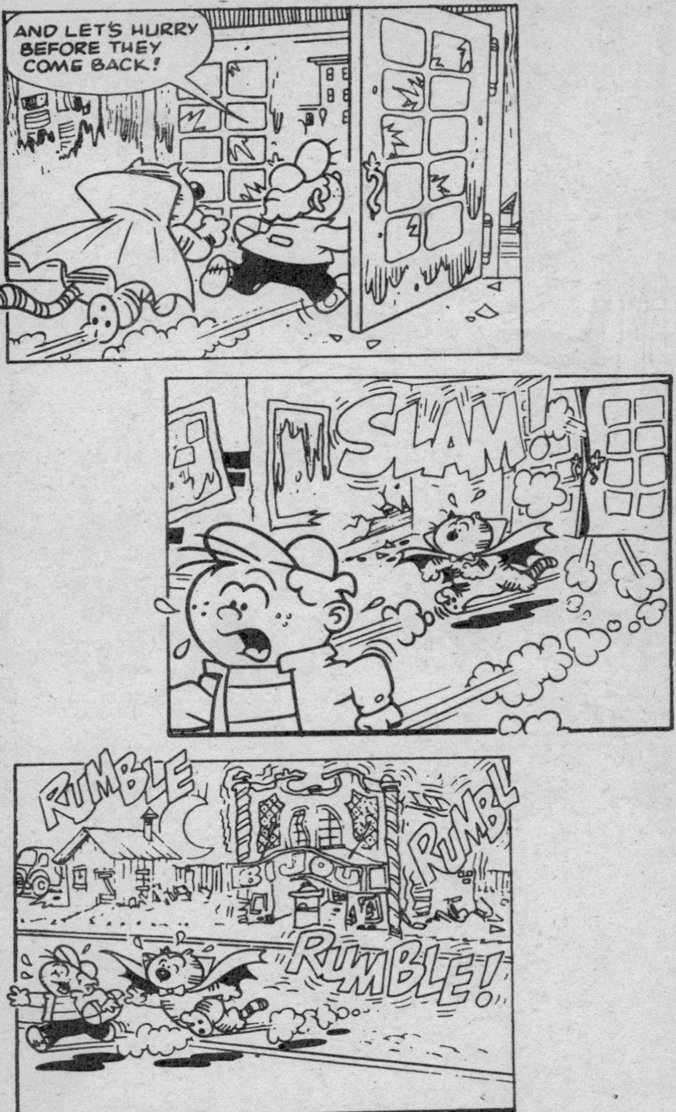
AND LET'S HURRY BEFORE THEY COME BACK!
SLAM!
RUMBLE
BIJOU
RUMBL
RUMBLE!

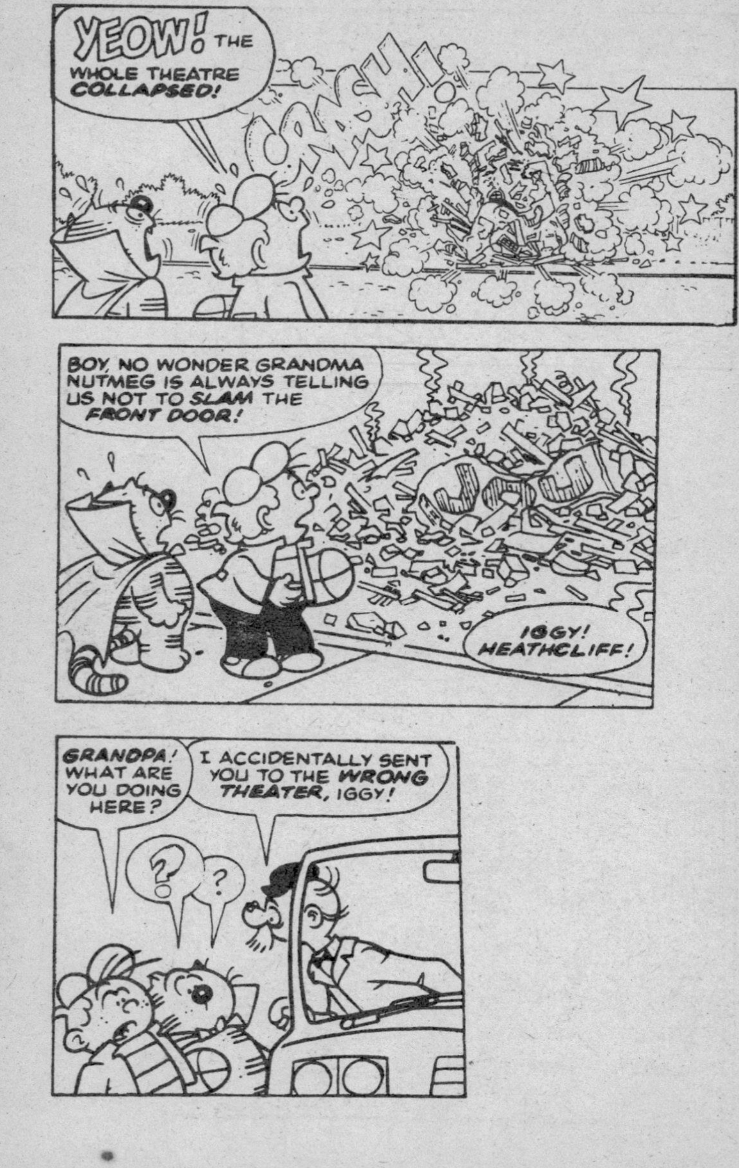
YEOW! THE WHOLE THEATRE COLLAPSED!
BOY, NO WONDER GRANDMA NUTMEG IS ALWAYS TELLING US NOT TO SLAM THE FRONT DOOR!
IGGY! HEATHCLIFF!
GRANDPA! WHAT ARE YOU DOING HERE?
I ACCIDENTALLY SENT YOU TO THE WRONG THEATER, IGGY!
?
?

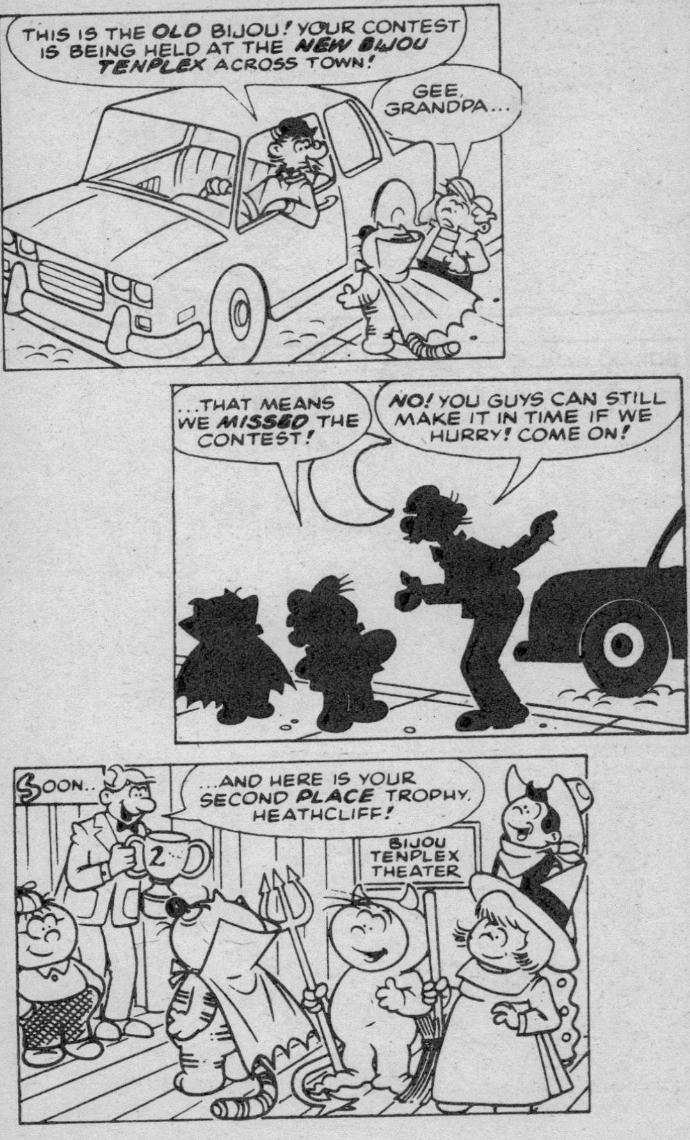
THIS IS THE OLD BIJOU! YOUR CONTEST IS BEING HELD AT THE NEW BIJOU TENPLEX ACROSS TOWN!
GEE, GRANDPA...
...THAT MEANS WE MISSED THE CONTEST!
NO! YOU GUYS CAN STILL MAKE IT IN TIME IF WE HURRY! COME ON!
SOON..
...AND HERE IS YOUR SECOND PLACE TROPHY, HEATHCLIFF!
2
BIJOU TENPLEX THEATER

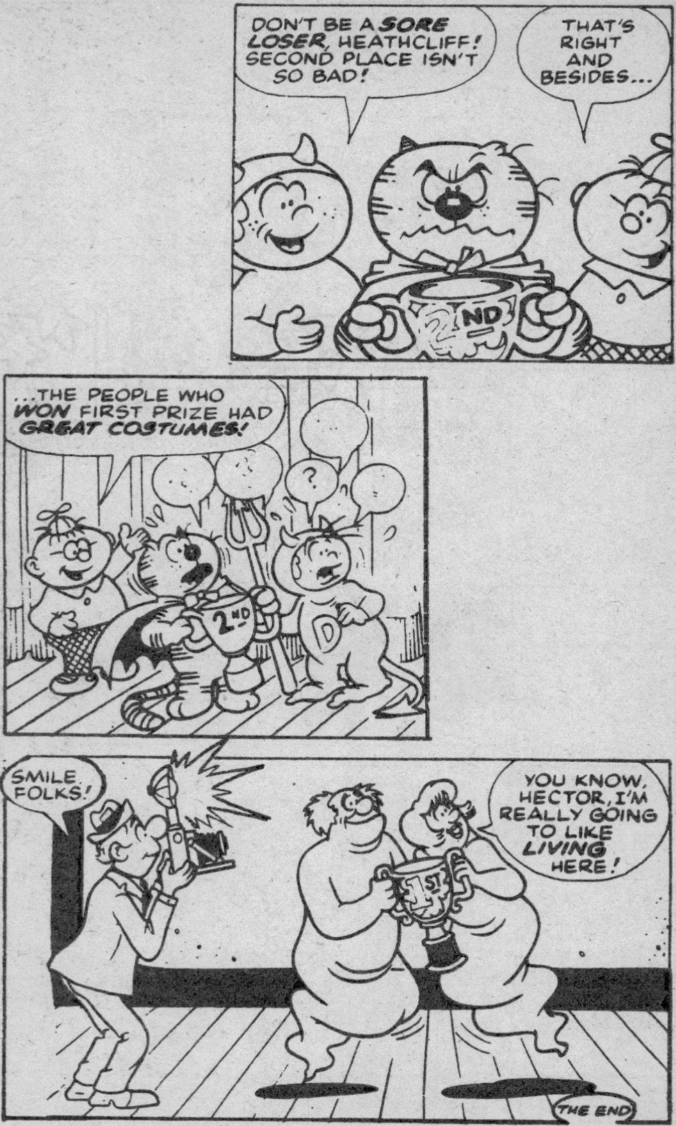
DON'T BE A SORE LOSER, HEATHCLIFF! SECOND PLACE ISN'T SO BAD!
THAT'S RIGHT AND BESIDES...
...THE PEOPLE WHO WON FIRST PRIZE HAD GREAT COSTUMES!
?
2ND
D
SMILE FOLKS!
YOU KNOW, HECTOR, I'M REALLY GOING TO LIKE LIVING HERE!
1ST
THE END

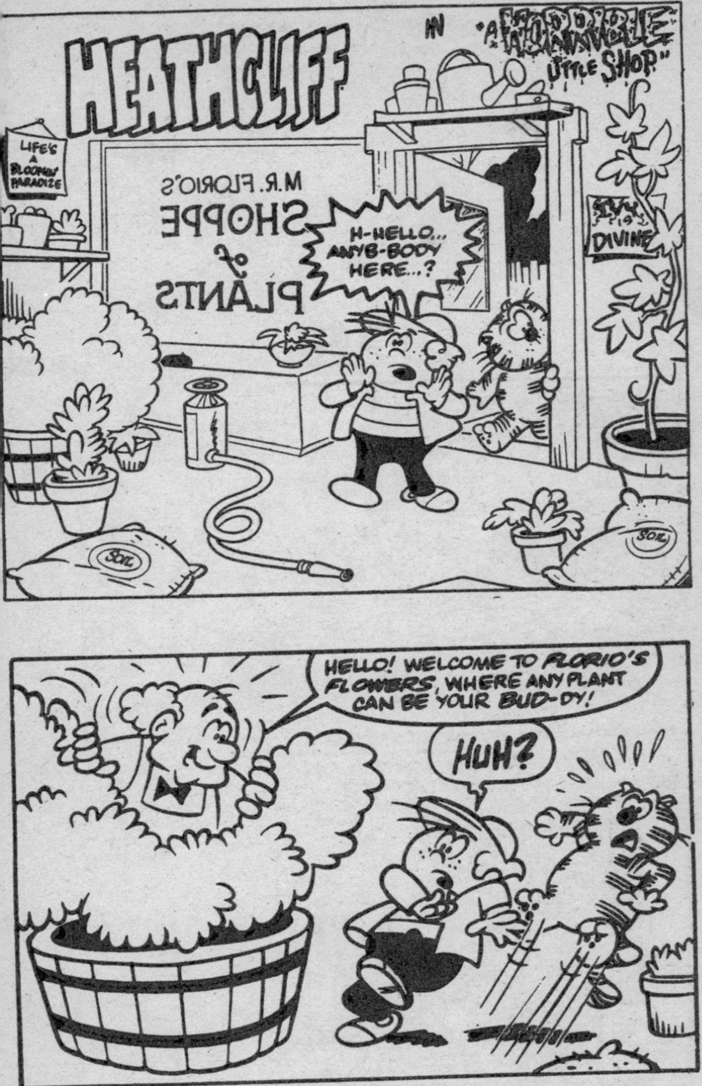
HEATHCLIFF
IN
"A HORRIBLE LITTLE SHOP"
LIFE'S A BLOOMIN' PARADIZE
M.R. FLORIO'S SHOPPE of PLANTS
IVY IS DIVINE
H-HELLO... ANYB-BODY HERE...?
SOIL
SOIL
HELLO! WELCOME TO FLORIO'S FLOWERS, WHERE ANY PLANT CAN BE YOUR BUD-DY!
HUH?

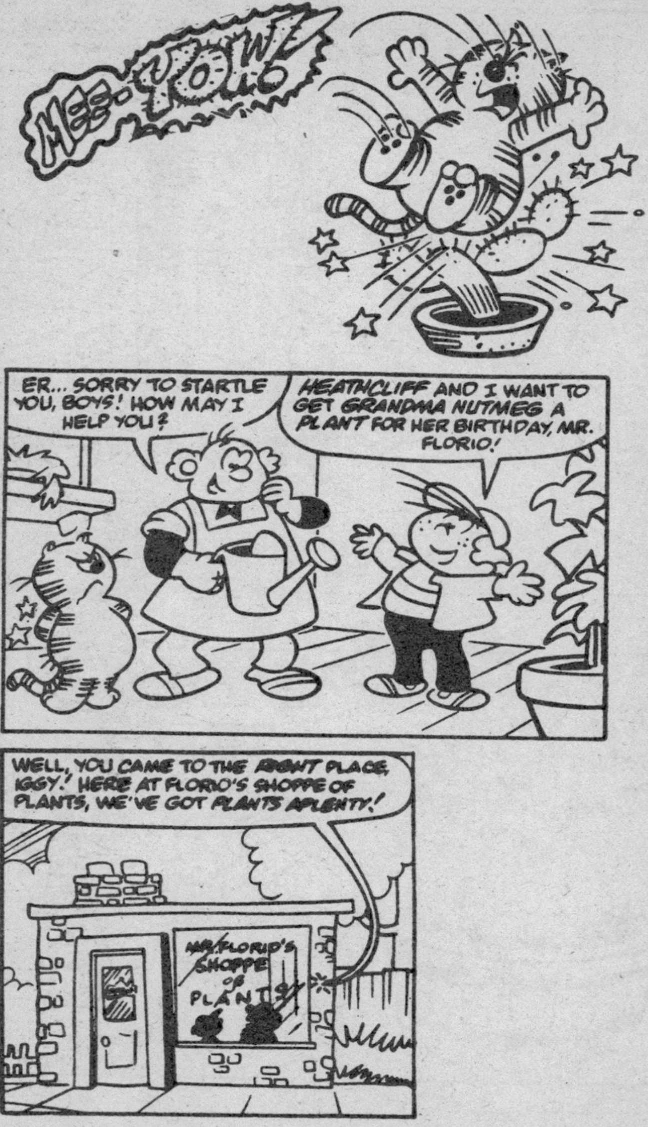
MEE-YOW!
ER... SORRY TO STARTLE YOU, BOYS! HOW MAY I HELP YOU?
HEATHCLIFF AND I WANT TO GET GRANDMA NUTMEG A PLANT FOR HER BIRTHDAY, MR. FLORIO!
WELL, YOU CAME TO THE RIGHT PLACE, IGGY! HERE AT FLORIO'S SHOPPE OF PLANTS, WE'VE GOT PLANTS APLENTY!
MR. FLORIO'S SHOPPE OF PLANTS

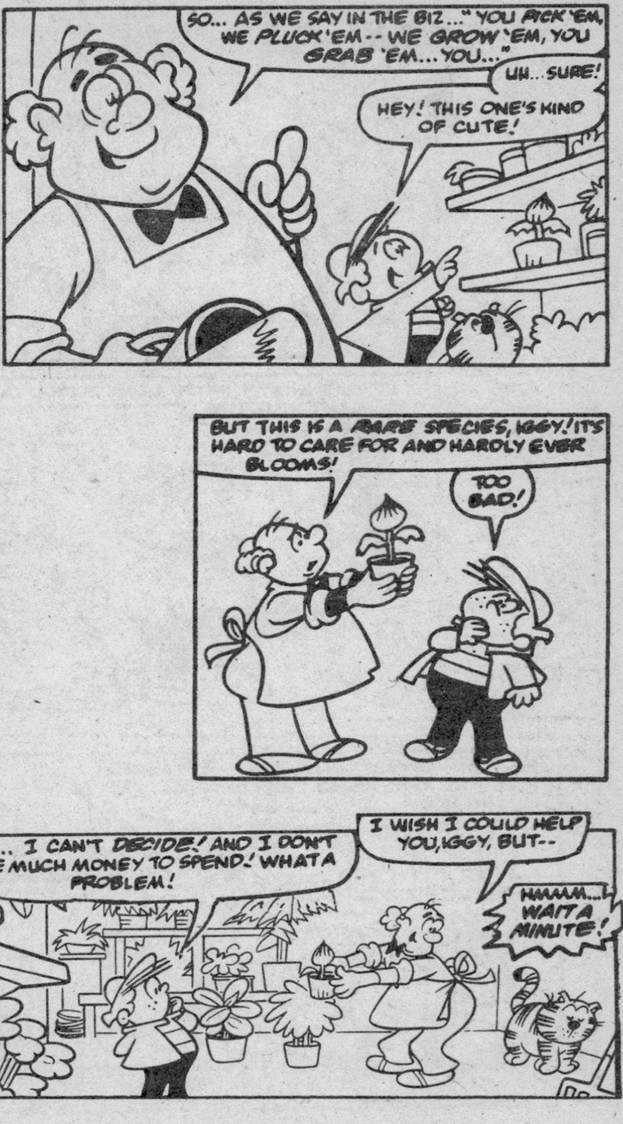
SO... AS WE SAY IN THE BIZ..."YOU PICK 'EM, WE PLUCK 'EM -- WE GROW 'EM, YOU GRAB 'EM... YOU..."
UH... SURE!
HEY! THIS ONE'S KIND OF CUTE!
BUT THIS IS A RARE SPECIES, IGGY! IT'S HARD TO CARE FOR AND HARDLY EVER BLOOMS!
TOO BAD!
GEE... I CAN'T DECIDE! AND I DON'T HAVE MUCH MONEY TO SPEND! WHAT A PROBLEM!
I WISH I COULD HELP YOU, IGGY, BUT--
HMMMM... WAIT A MINUTE!

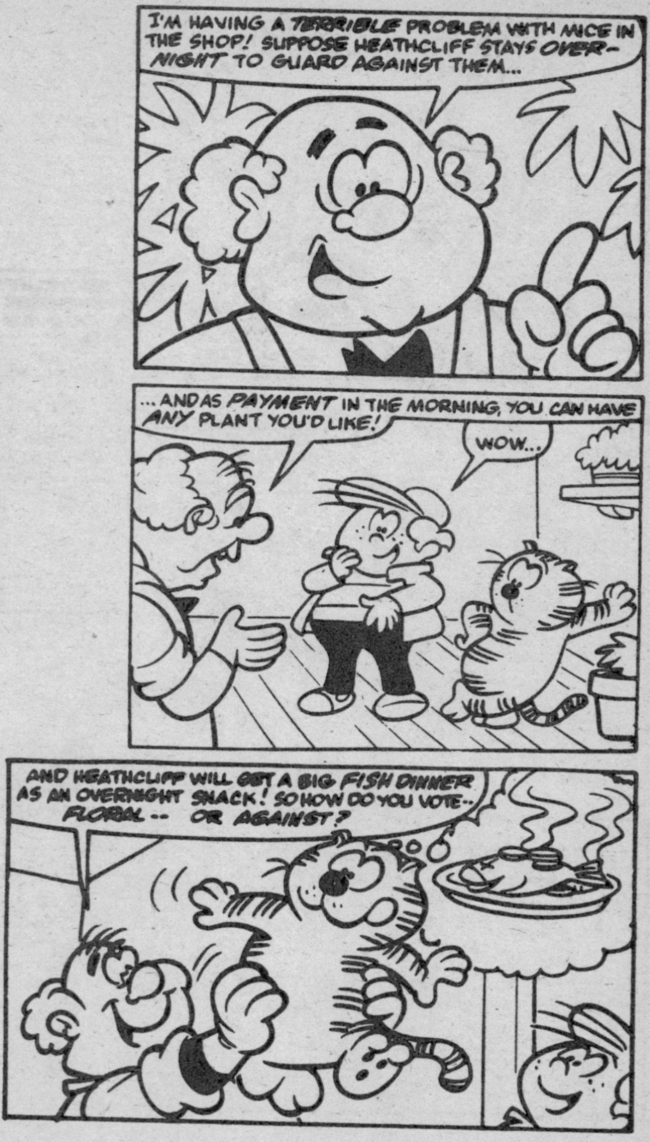
I'M HAVING A TERRIBLE PROBLEM WITH MICE IN THE SHOP! SUPPOSE HEATHCLIFF STAYS OVER-NIGHT TO GUARD AGAINST THEM...
...AND AS PAYMENT IN THE MORNING, YOU CAN HAVE ANY PLANT YOU'D LIKE!
WOW...
AND HEATHCLIFF WILL GET A BIG FISH DINNER AS AN OVERNIGHT SNACK! SO HOW DO YOU VOTE-- FLORAL -- OR AGAINST?

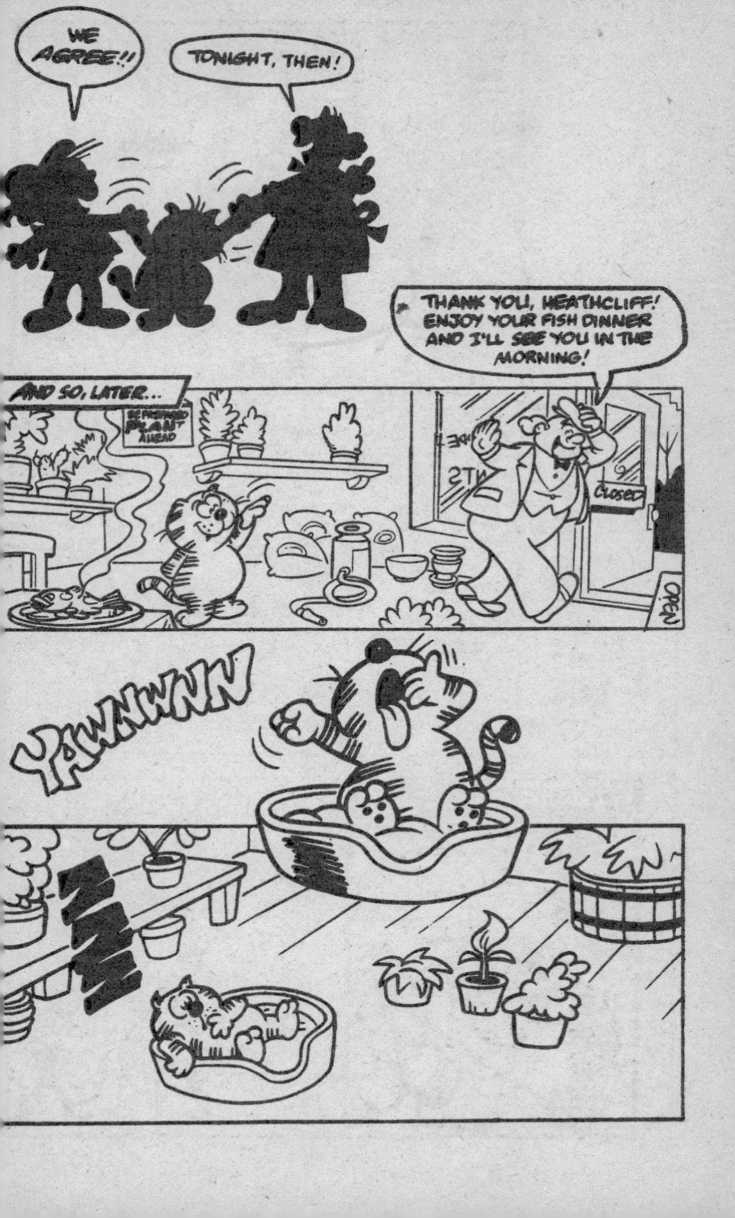

WE AGREE!!
TONIGHT, THEN!
THANK YOU, HEATHCLIFF! ENJOY YOUR FISH DINNER AND I'LL SEE YOU IN THE MORNING!
AND SO, LATER...
PLANT AHEAD
CLOSED
OPEN
YAWNWNN

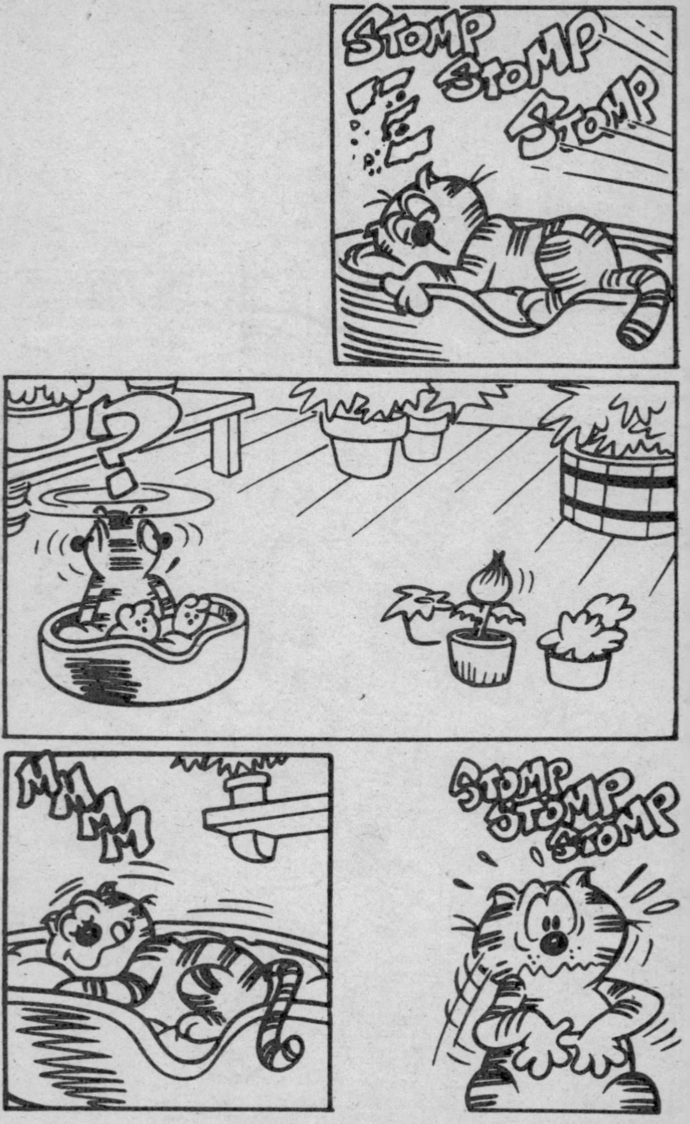
STOMP STOMP STOMP
MMMM
STOMP STOMP STOMP

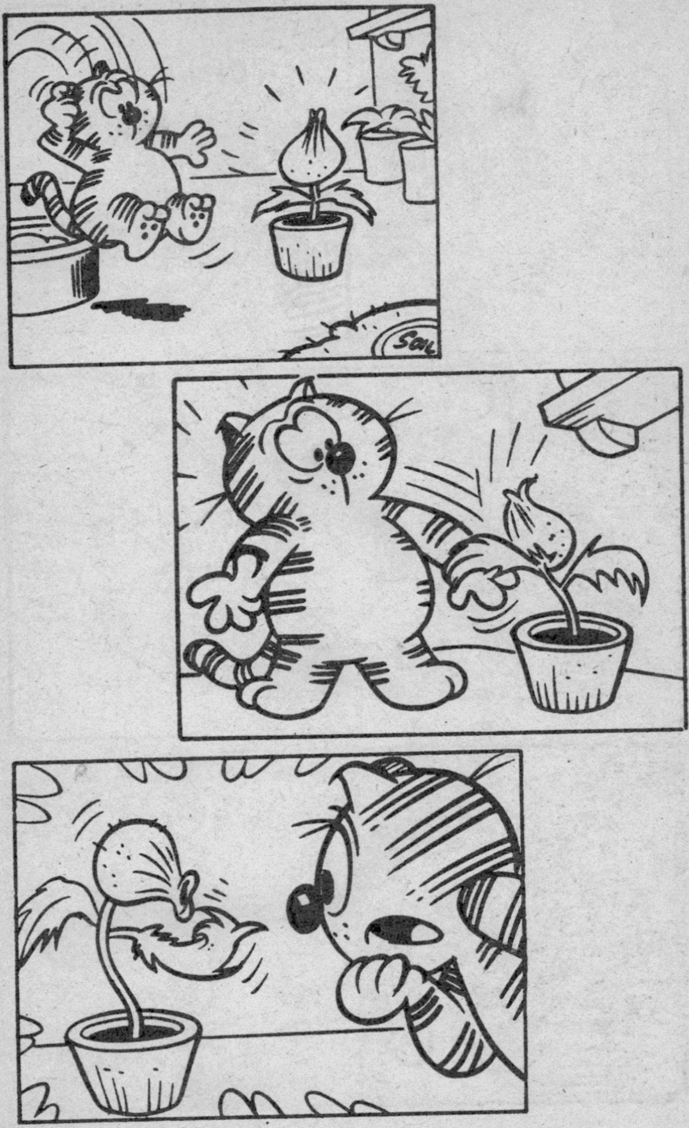

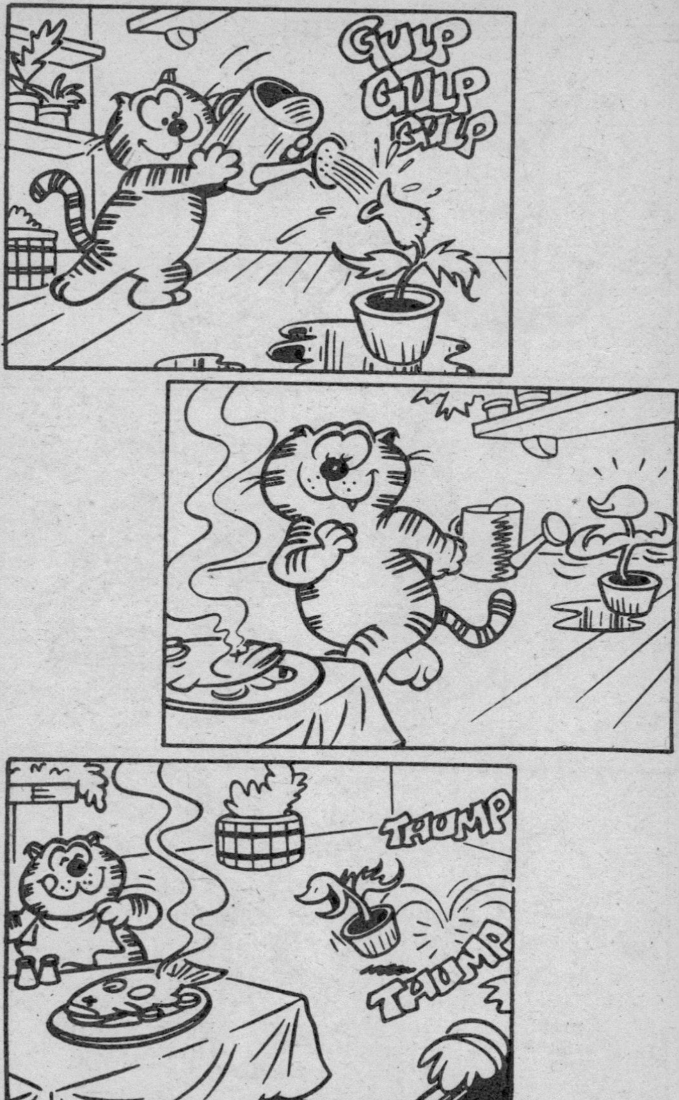
GULP
GULP
GULP
THUMP
THUMP

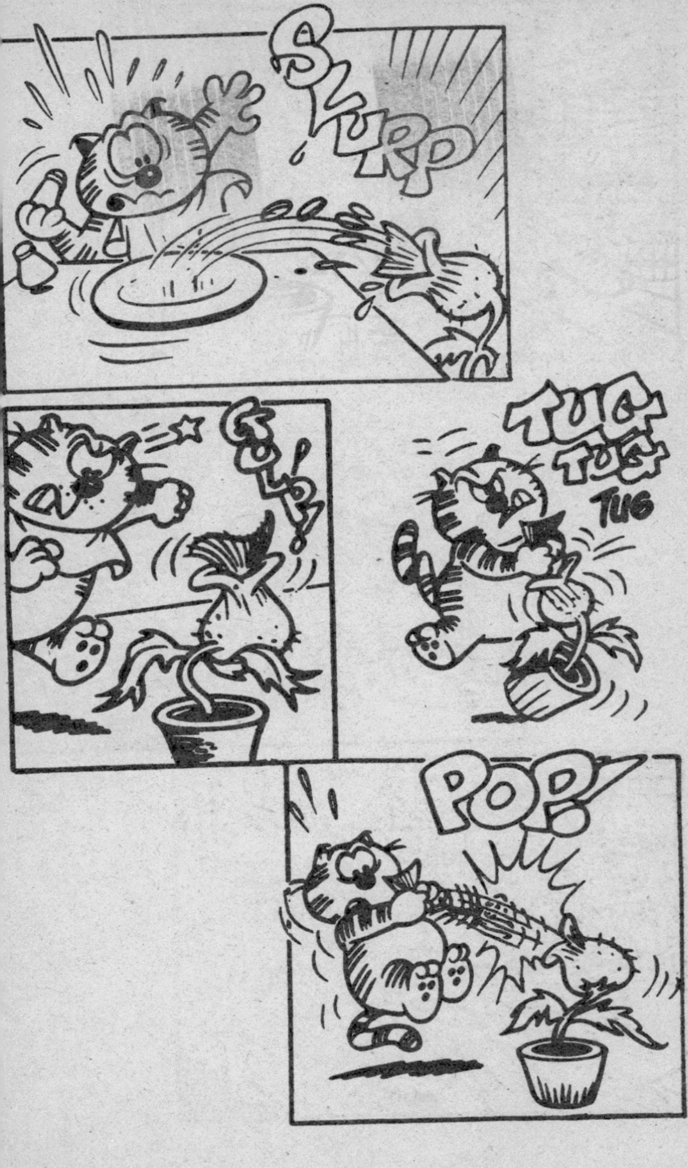
SLURP
GULP!
TUG
TUG
TUG
POP!

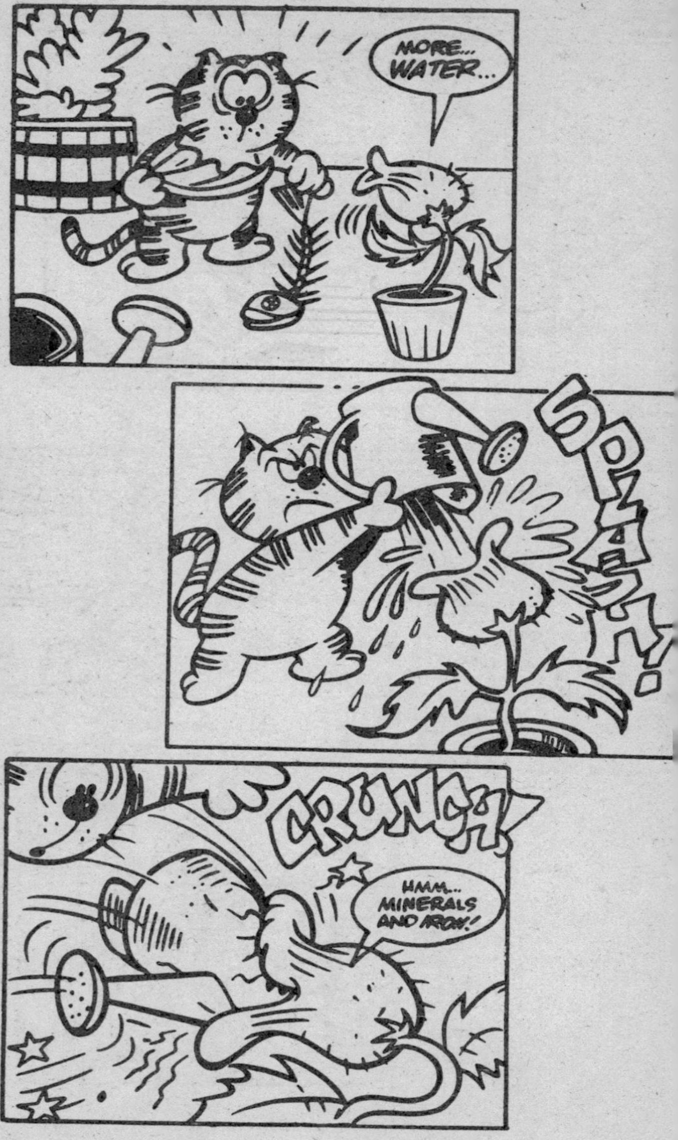
MORE... WATER...
SPLASH!
CRUNCH
HMM... MINERALS AND IRON!

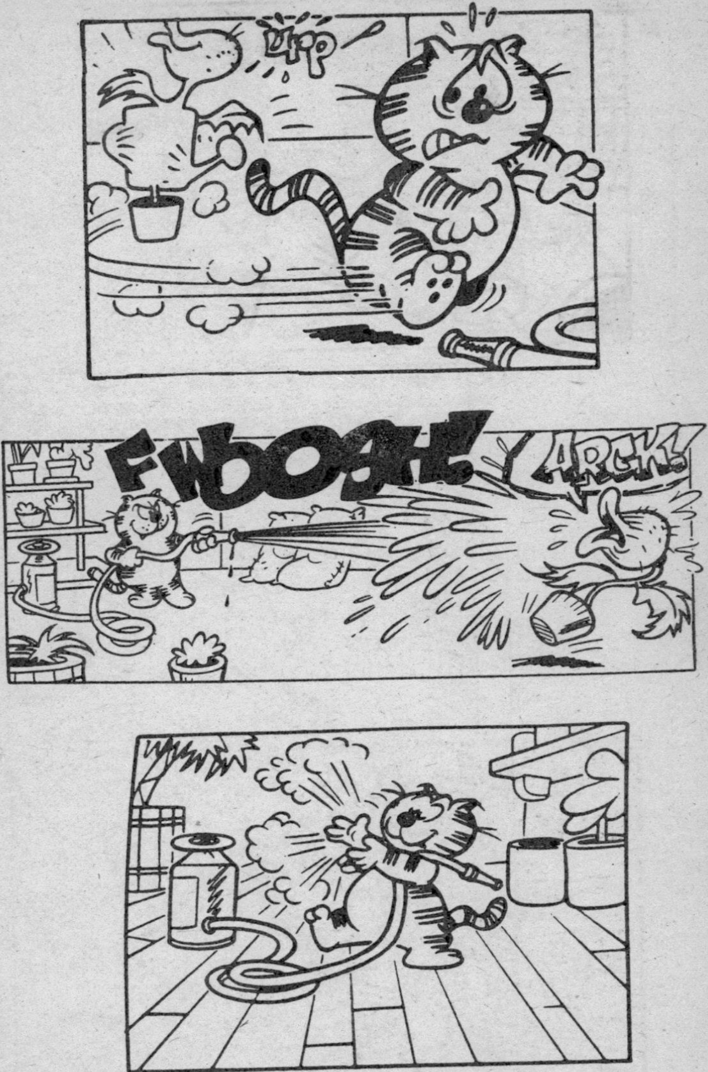
YIPP
FWOSH!
ARCK!

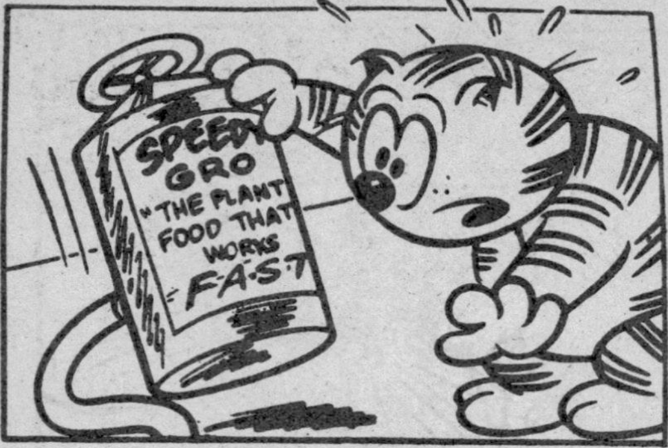
SPEED
GRO
"THE PLANT
FOOD THAT
WORKS
F-A-S-T"

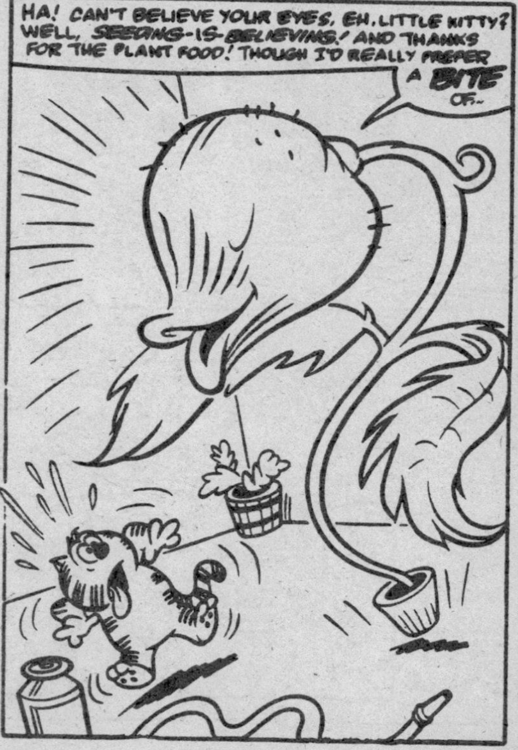
HA! CAN'T BELIEVE YOUR EYES, EH, LITTLE KITTY? WELL, SEEING-IS-BELIEVING! AND THANKS FOR THE PLANT FOOD! THOUGH I'D REALLY PREFER
A BITE OF...

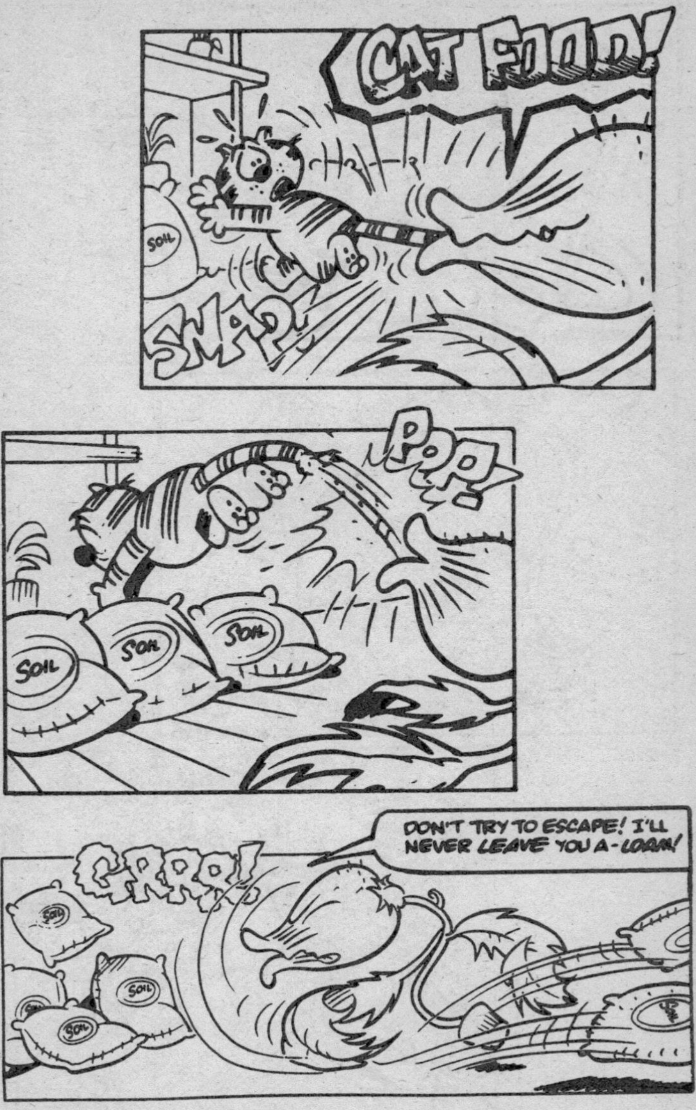
CAT FOOD!
SNAP!
SOIL
POP!
SOIL
SOIL
SOIL
DON'T TRY TO ESCAPE! I'LL NEVER *LEAVE* YOU A-*LOAM*!
GRRR!
SOIL
SOIL
SOIL

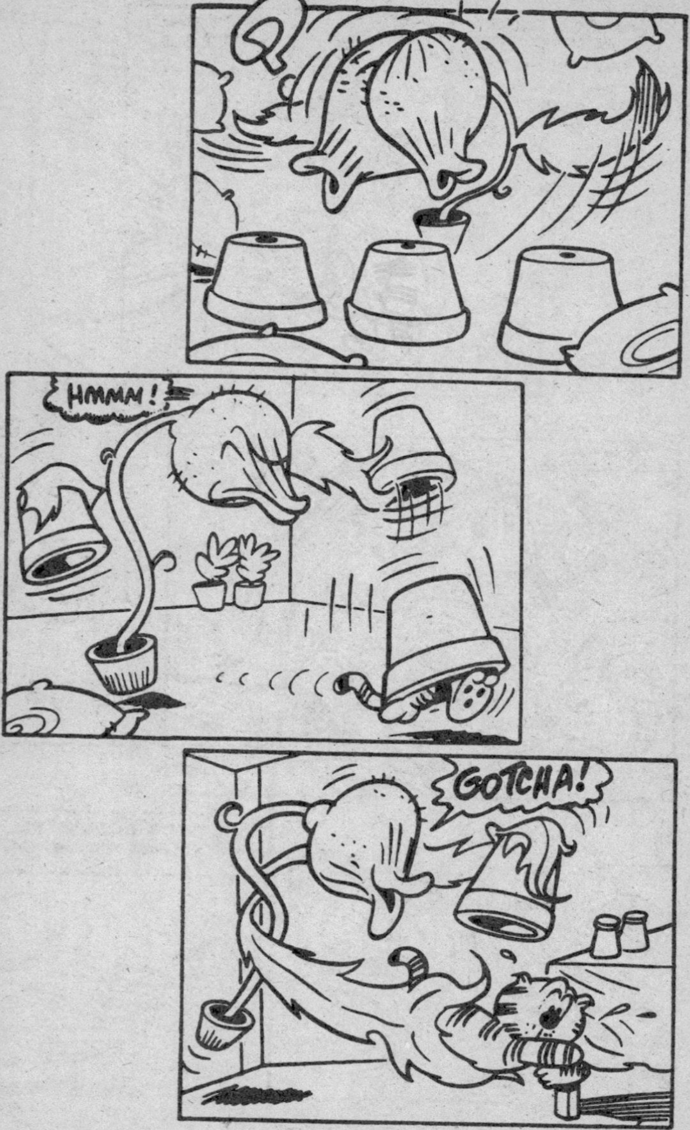
HMMM!
GOTCHA!

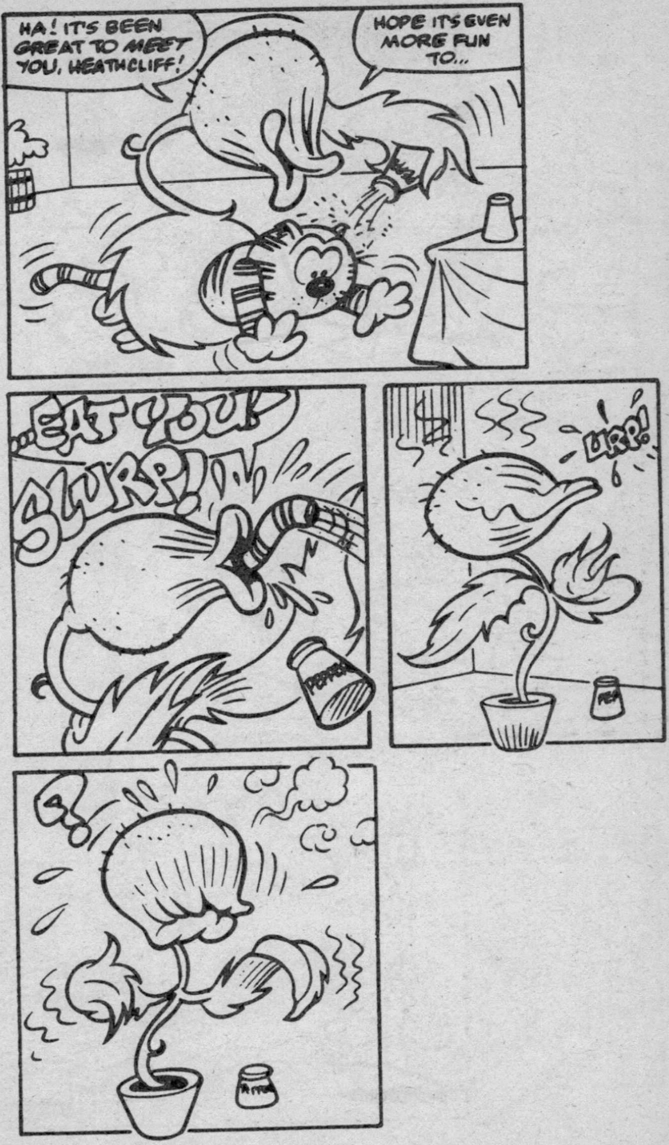
HA! IT'S BEEN GREAT TO MEET YOU, HEATHCLIFF!
HOPE IT'S EVEN MORE FUN TO...
...EAT YOU!
SLURP!
PEPPER
URP!

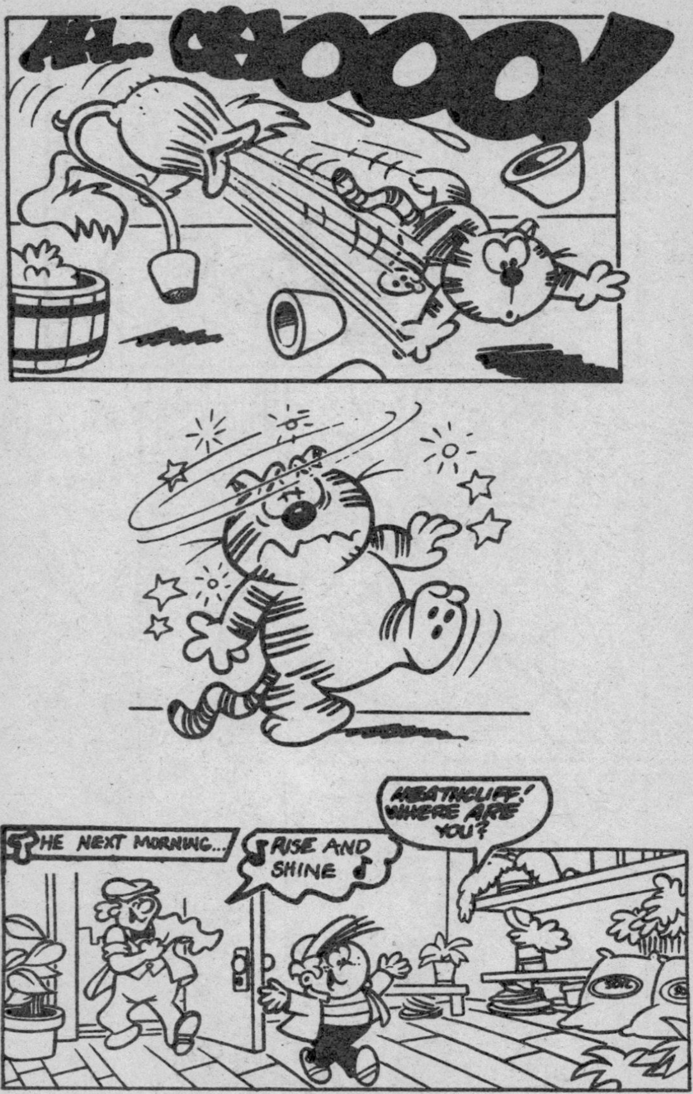
AH... CHOOO!
THE NEXT MORNING...
RISE AND SHINE
HEATHCLIFF! WHERE ARE YOU?

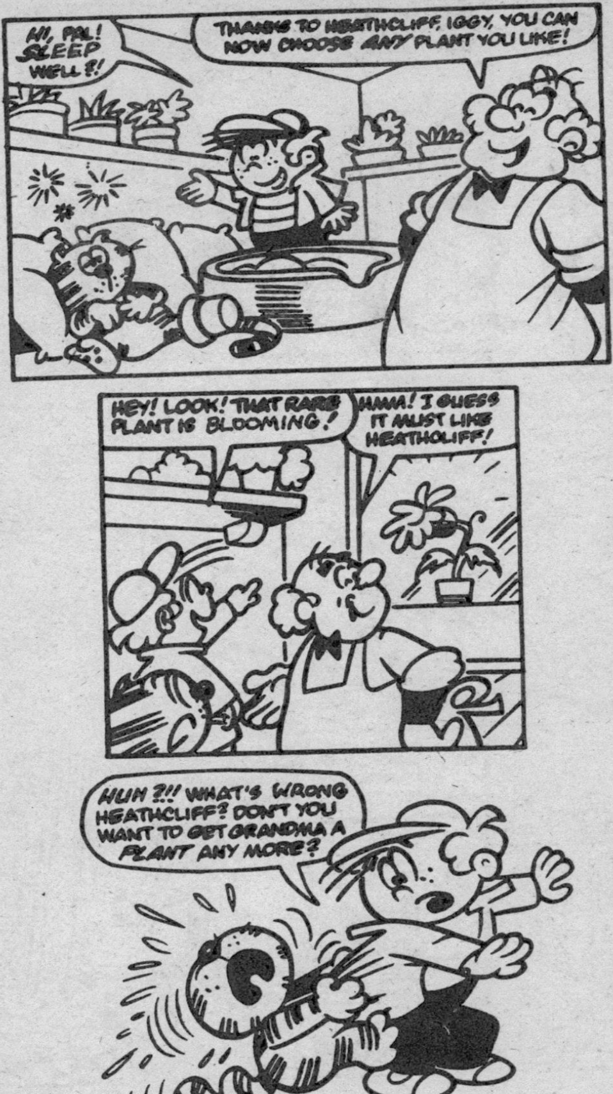
HI, PAL! SLEEP WELL?!
THANKS TO HEATHCLIFF, IGGY, YOU CAN NOW CHOOSE ANY PLANT YOU LIKE!
HEY! LOOK! THAT RARE PLANT IS BLOOMING!
HMM! I GUESS IT MUST LIKE HEATHCLIFF!
HUH?!! WHAT'S WRONG HEATHCLIFF? DON'T YOU WANT TO GET GRANDMA A PLANT ANY MORE?

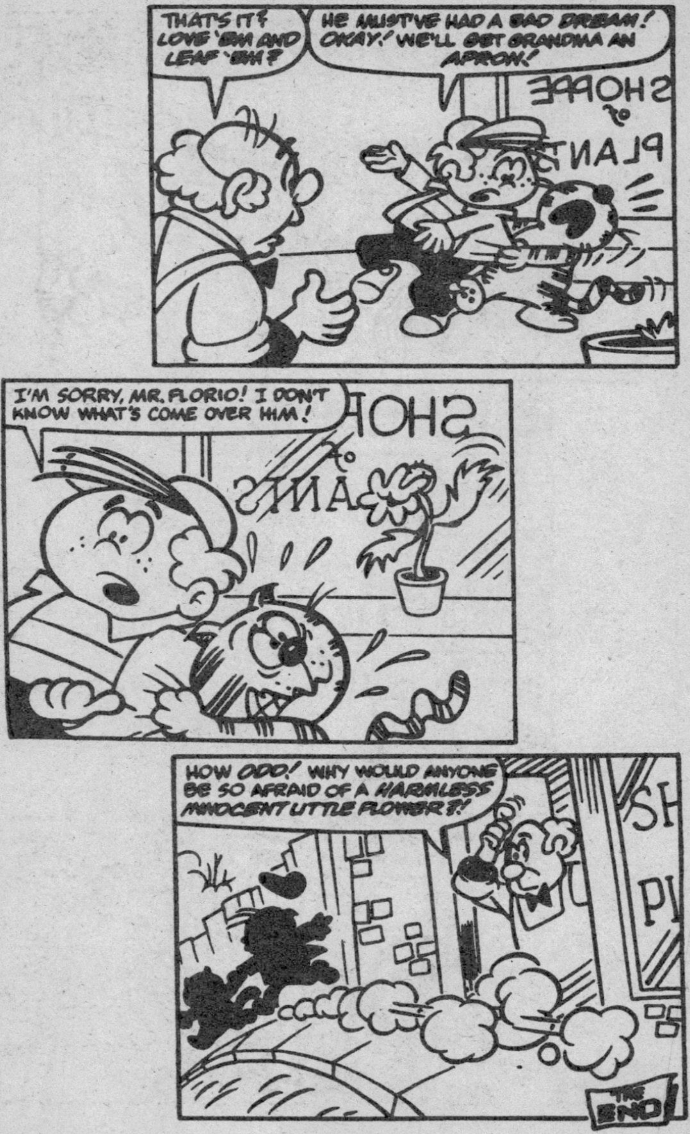
THAT'S IT? LOVE 'EM AND LEAF 'EM?
HE MUST'VE HAD A BAD DREAM! OKAY! WE'LL GET GRANDMA AN APRON!
I'M SORRY, MR. FLORIO! I DON'T KNOW WHAT'S COME OVER HIM!
HOW ODD! WHY WOULD ANYONE BE SO AFRAID OF A HARMLESS INNOCENT LITTLE FLOWER?!
THE END

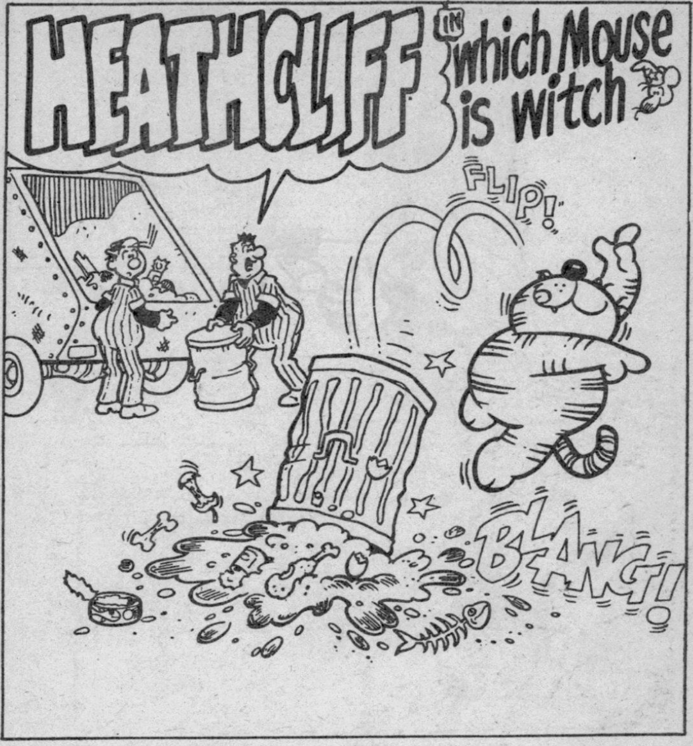
HEATHCLIFF in which Mouse is witch
FLIP!
BLANG!

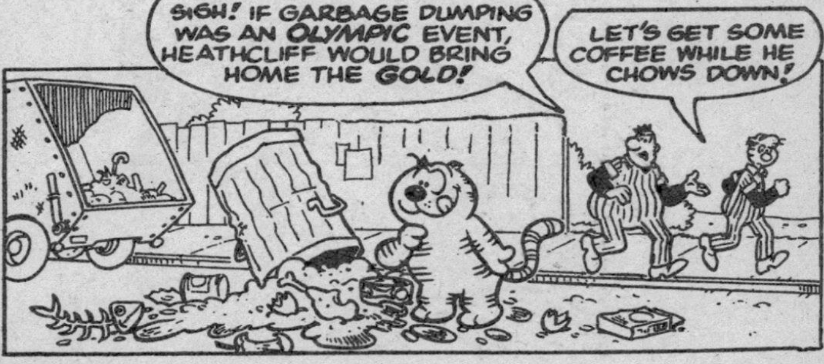
SIGH! IF GARBAGE DUMPING WAS AN OLYMPIC EVENT, HEATHCLIFF WOULD BRING HOME THE GOLD!
LET'S GET SOME COFFEE WHILE HE CHOWS DOWN!

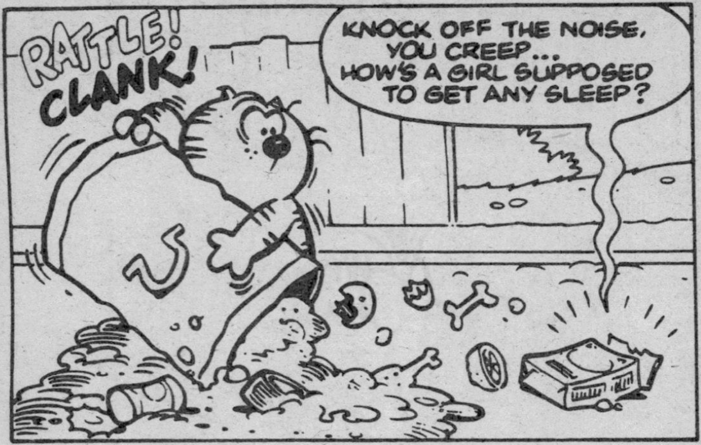
RATTLE!
CLANK!
KNOCK OFF THE NOISE, YOU CREEP... HOW'S A GIRL SUPPOSED TO GET ANY SLEEP?

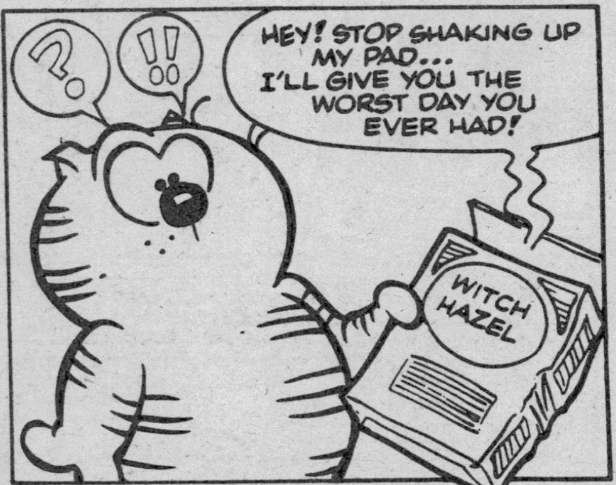
?
!!
HEY! STOP SHAKING UP MY PAD... I'LL GIVE YOU THE WORST DAY YOU EVER HAD!
WITCH HAZEL

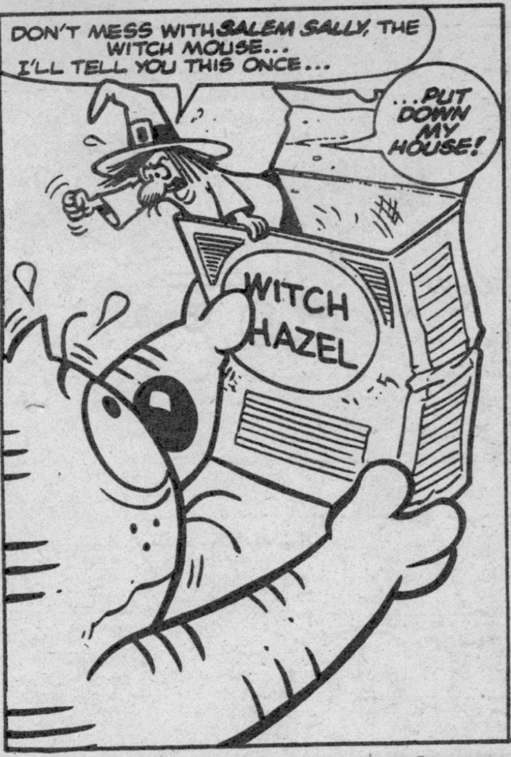
DON'T MESS WITH SALEM SALLY, THE WITCH MOUSE... I'LL TELL YOU THIS ONCE...
...PUT DOWN MY HOUSE!
WITCH HAZEL

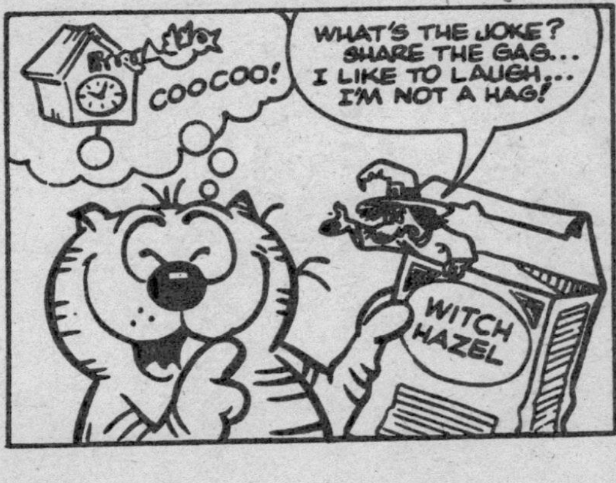
COOCOO!
WHAT'S THE JOKE? SHARE THE GAG... I LIKE TO LAUGH... I'M NOT A HAG!
WITCH HAZEL

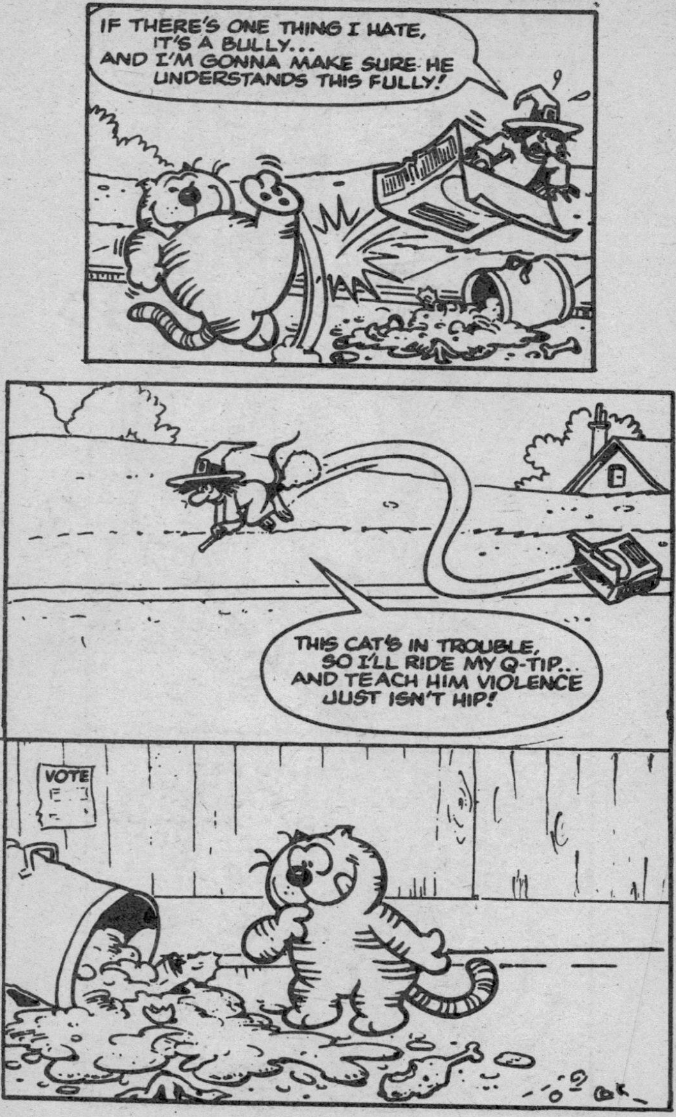
IF THERE'S ONE THING I HATE, IT'S A BULLY... AND I'M GONNA MAKE SURE HE UNDERSTANDS THIS FULLY!
THIS CAT'S IN TROUBLE, SO I'LL RIDE MY Q-TIP... AND TEACH HIM VIOLENCE JUST ISN'T HIP!
VOTE

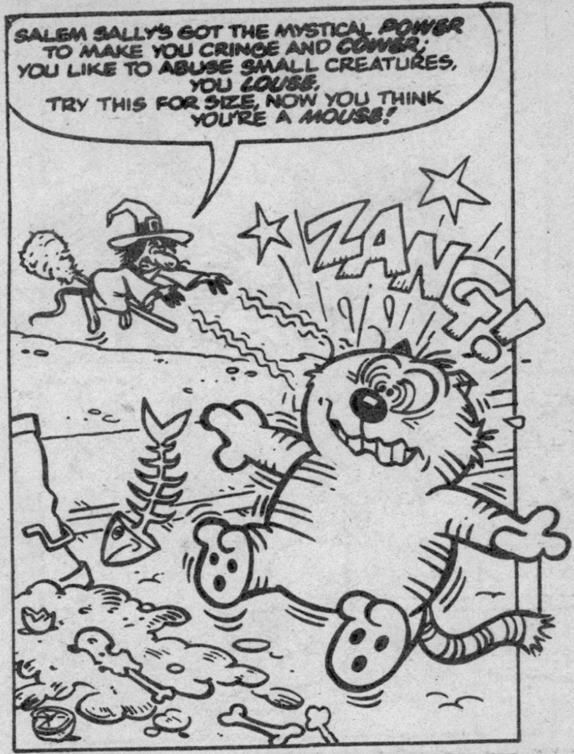
SALEM SALLY'S GOT THE MYSTICAL POWER
TO MAKE YOU CRINGE AND COWER;
YOU LIKE TO ABUSE SMALL CREATURES,
YOU LOUSE,
TRY THIS FOR SIZE, NOW YOU THINK
YOU'RE A MOUSE!
ZANG!

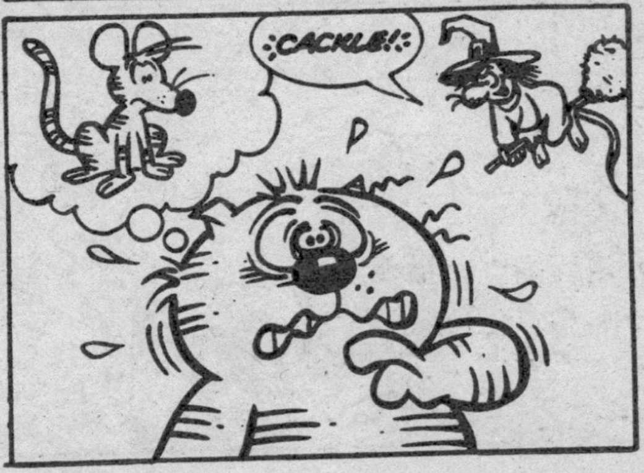
CACKLE!

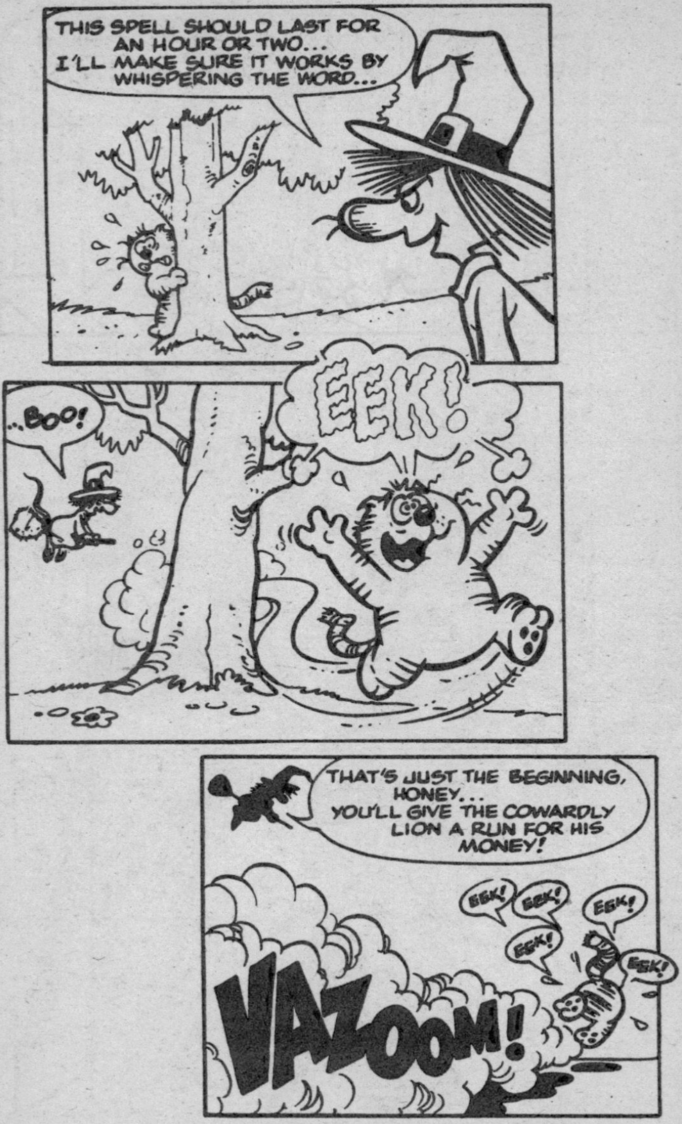
THIS SPELL SHOULD LAST FOR AN HOUR OR TWO... I'LL MAKE SURE IT WORKS BY WHISPERING THE WORD...
...BOO!
EEK!
THAT'S JUST THE BEGINNING, HONEY... YOU'LL GIVE THE COWARDLY LION A RUN FOR HIS MONEY!
EEK!
EEK!
EEK!
EEK!
EEK!
VAZOOM!

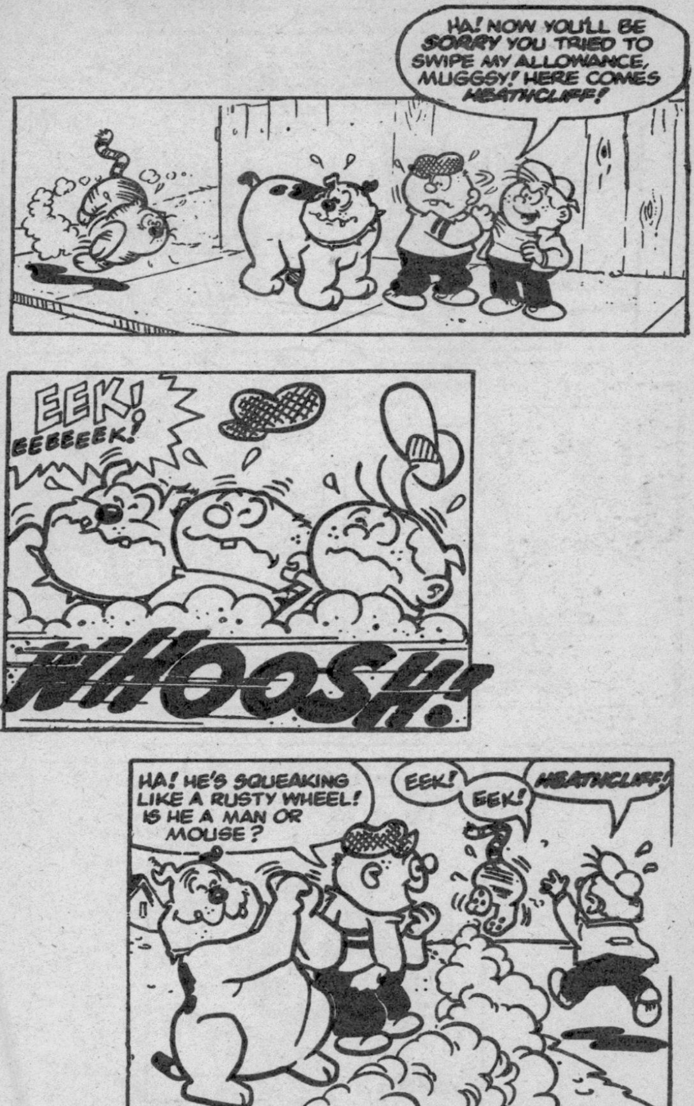

HA! NOW YOU'LL BE SORRY YOU TRIED TO SWIPE MY ALLOWANCE, MUGGSY! HERE COMES HEATHCLIFF!
EEK!
EEEEEEK!
WHOOSH!
HA! HE'S SQUEAKING LIKE A RUSTY WHEEL! IS HE A MAN OR MOUSE?
EEK!
EEK!
HEATHCLIFF!

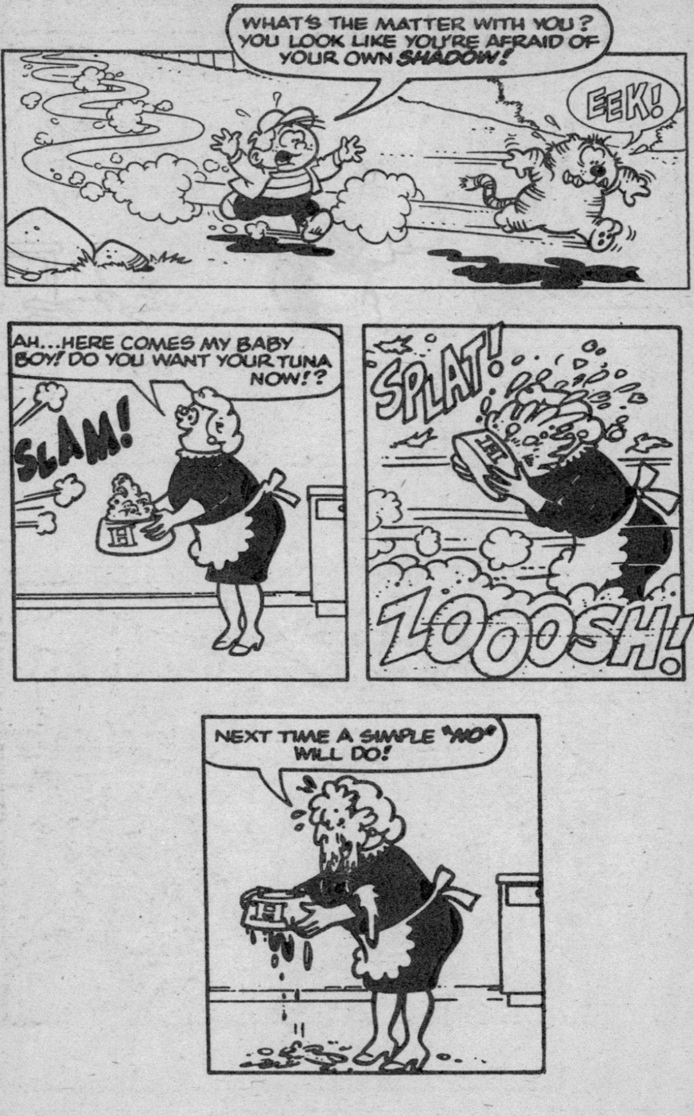
WHAT'S THE MATTER WITH YOU? YOU LOOK LIKE YOU'RE AFRAID OF YOUR OWN SHADOW!
EEK!
AH...HERE COMES MY BABY BOY! DO YOU WANT YOUR TUNA NOW!?
SLAM!
SPLAT!
ZOOOSH!
NEXT TIME A SIMPLE "NO" WILL DO!

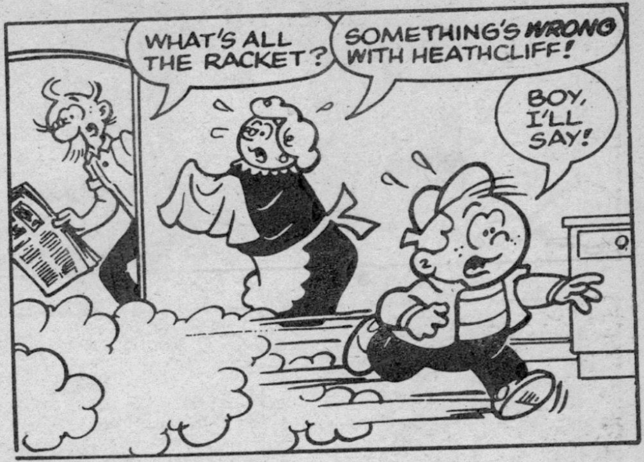
WHAT'S ALL THE RACKET?
SOMETHING'S WRONG WITH HEATHCLIFF!
BOY, I'LL SAY!

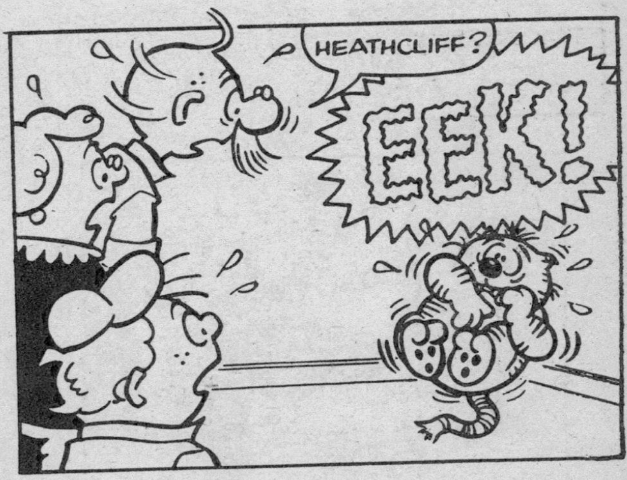
HEATHCLIFF?
EEK!

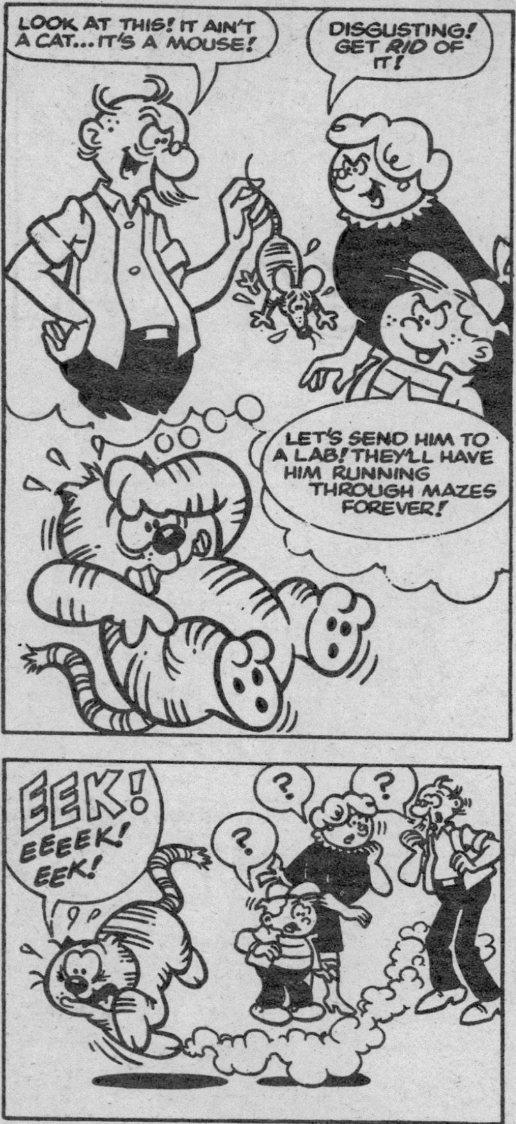
LOOK AT THIS! IT AIN'T A CAT...IT'S A MOUSE!
DISGUSTING! GET RID OF IT!
LET'S SEND HIM TO A LAB! THEY'LL HAVE HIM RUNNING THROUGH MAZES FOREVER!
EEK! EEEEK! EEK!
?
?
?

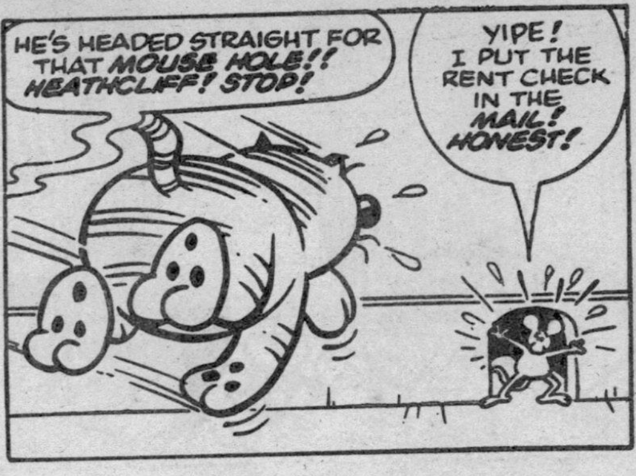
HE'S HEADED STRAIGHT FOR THAT MOUSE HOLE!! HEATHCLIFF! STOP!
YIPE! I PUT THE RENT CHECK IN THE MAIL! HONEST!

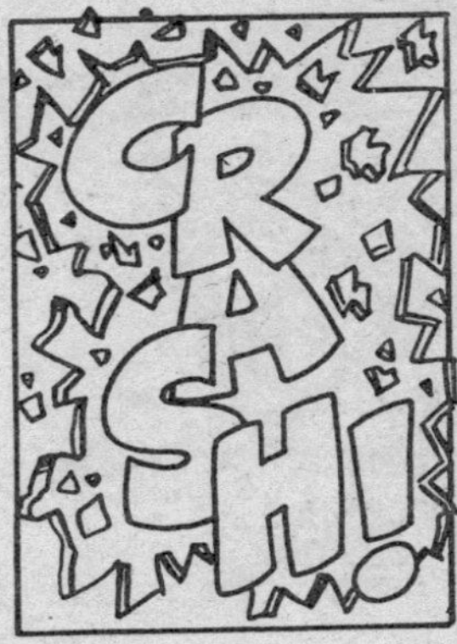
CRASH!

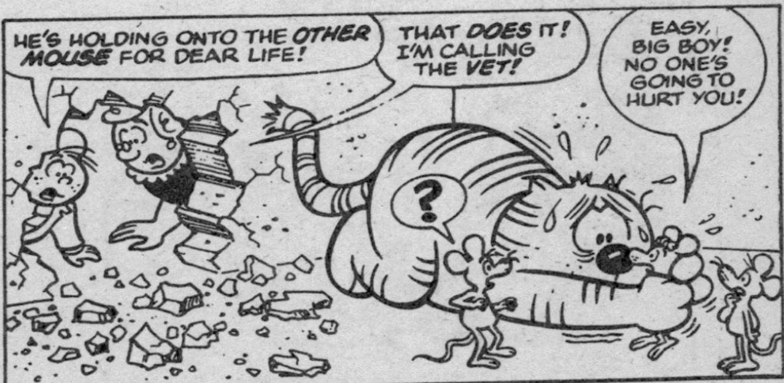
HE'S HOLDING ONTO THE OTHER MOUSE FOR DEAR LIFE!
THAT DOES IT! I'M CALLING THE VET!
EASY, BIG BOY! NO ONE'S GOING TO HURT YOU!
?

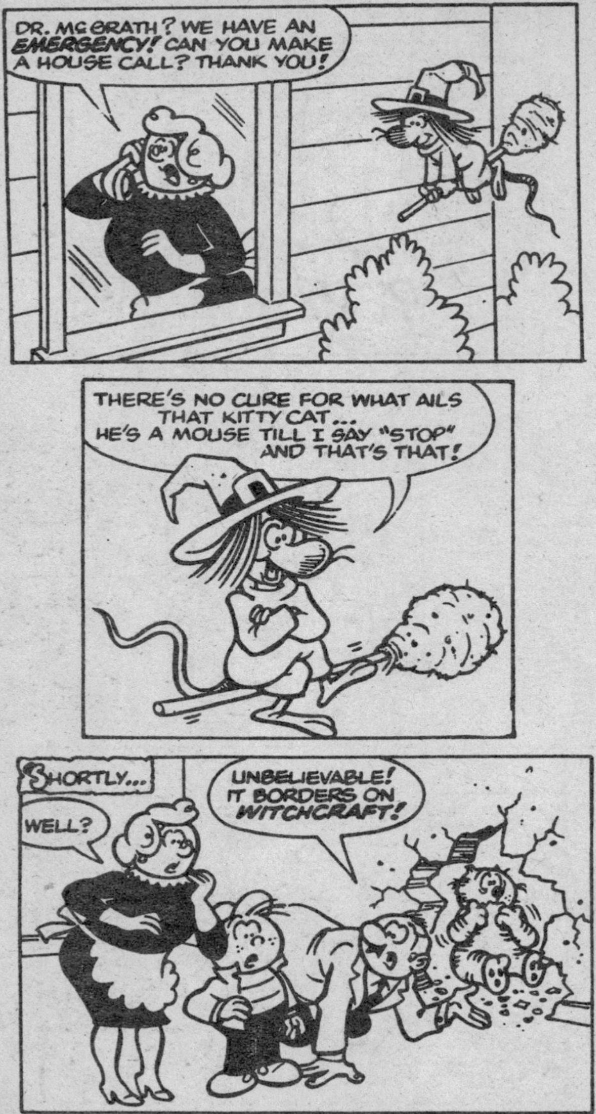
DR. McGRATH? WE HAVE AN EMERGENCY! CAN YOU MAKE A HOUSE CALL? THANK YOU!
THERE'S NO CURE FOR WHAT AILS THAT KITTY CAT... HE'S A MOUSE TILL I SAY "STOP" AND THAT'S THAT!
SHORTLY...
WELL?
UNBELIEVABLE! IT BORDERS ON WITCHCRAFT!

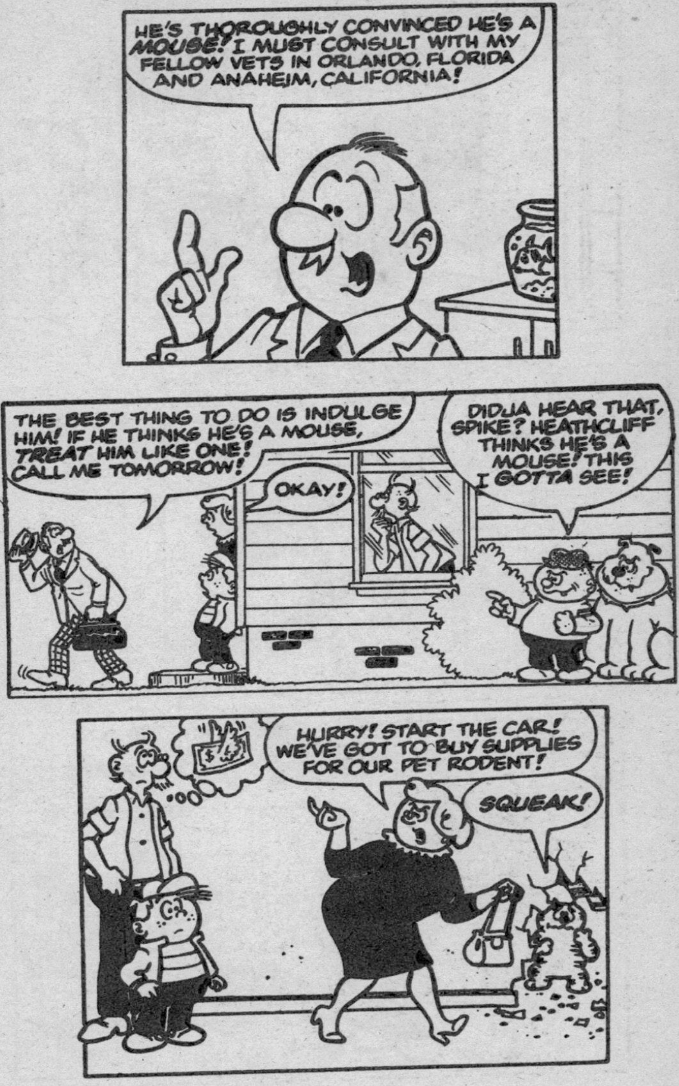
HE'S THOROUGHLY CONVINCED HE'S A MOUSE! I MUST CONSULT WITH MY FELLOW VETS IN ORLANDO, FLORIDA AND ANAHEIM, CALIFORNIA!
THE BEST THING TO DO IS INDULGE HIM! IF HE THINKS HE'S A MOUSE, TREAT HIM LIKE ONE! CALL ME TOMORROW!
OKAY!
DIDJA HEAR THAT, SPIKE? HEATHCLIFF THINKS HE'S A MOUSE! THIS I GOTTA SEE!
HURRY! START THE CAR! WE'VE GOT TO BUY SUPPLIES FOR OUR PET RODENT!
SQUEAK!

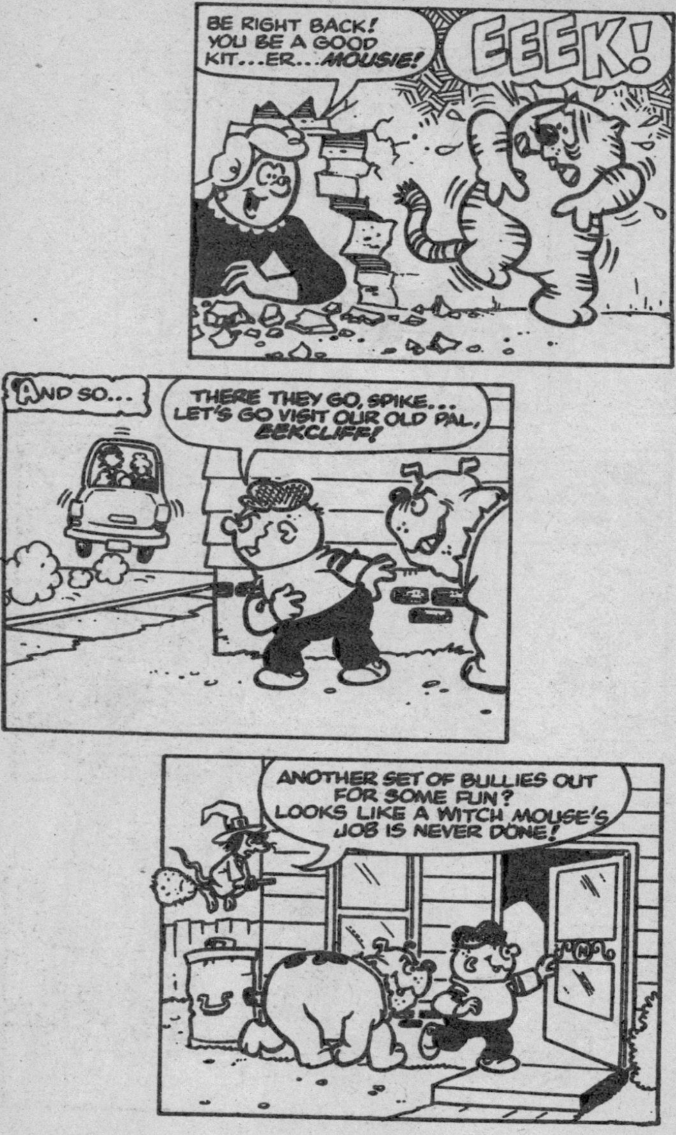
BE RIGHT BACK! YOU BE A GOOD KIT...ER...MOUSIE!
EEEK!
AND SO...
THERE THEY GO, SPIKE... LET'S GO VISIT OUR OLD PAL, EEKCLIFF!
ANOTHER SET OF BULLIES OUT FOR SOME FUN? LOOKS LIKE A WITCH MOUSE'S JOB IS NEVER DONE!

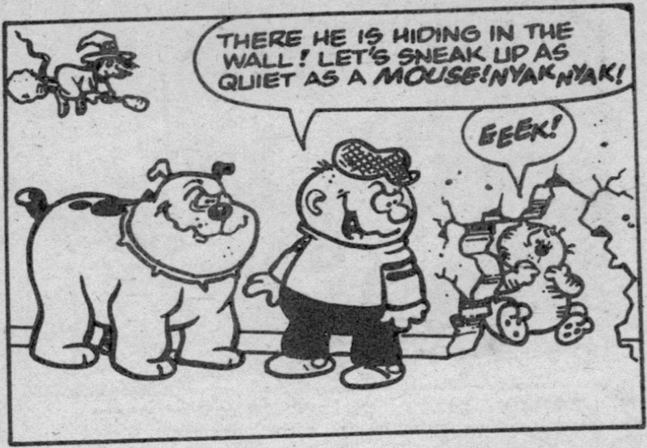
THERE HE IS HIDING IN THE WALL! LET'S SNEAK UP AS QUIET AS A MOUSE! NYAK NYAK!
EEEK!

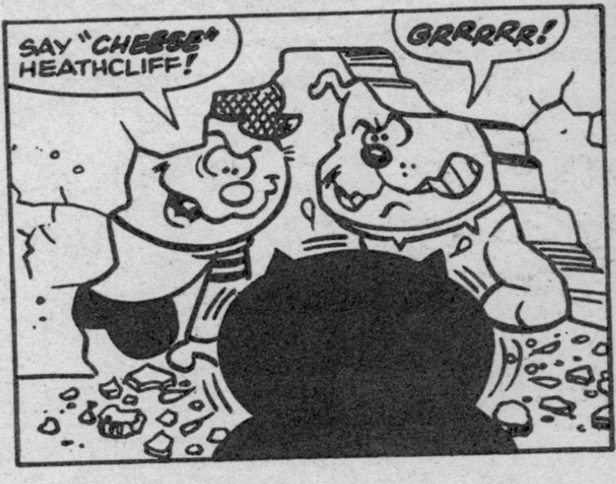
SAY "CHEESE" HEATHCLIFF!
GRRRRR!

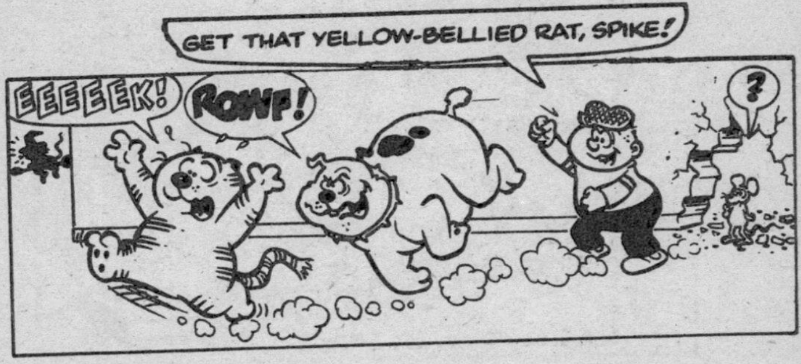
GET THAT YELLOW-BELLIED RAT, SPIKE!
EEEEEEK!
RONF!
?

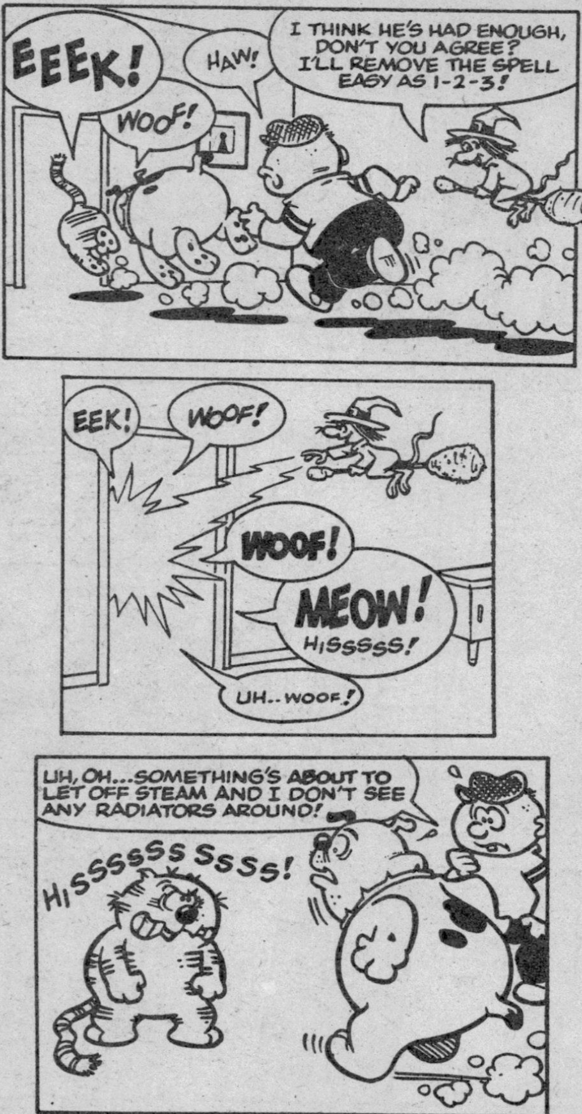
EEEK!
WOOF!
HAW!
I THINK HE'S HAD ENOUGH, DON'T YOU AGREE? I'LL REMOVE THE SPELL EASY AS 1-2-3!
EEK!
WOOF!
WOOF!
MEOW! HISSSSS!
UH.. WOOF!
UH, OH...SOMETHING'S ABOUT TO LET OFF STEAM AND I DON'T SEE ANY RADIATORS AROUND!
HISSSSSS SSSSS!

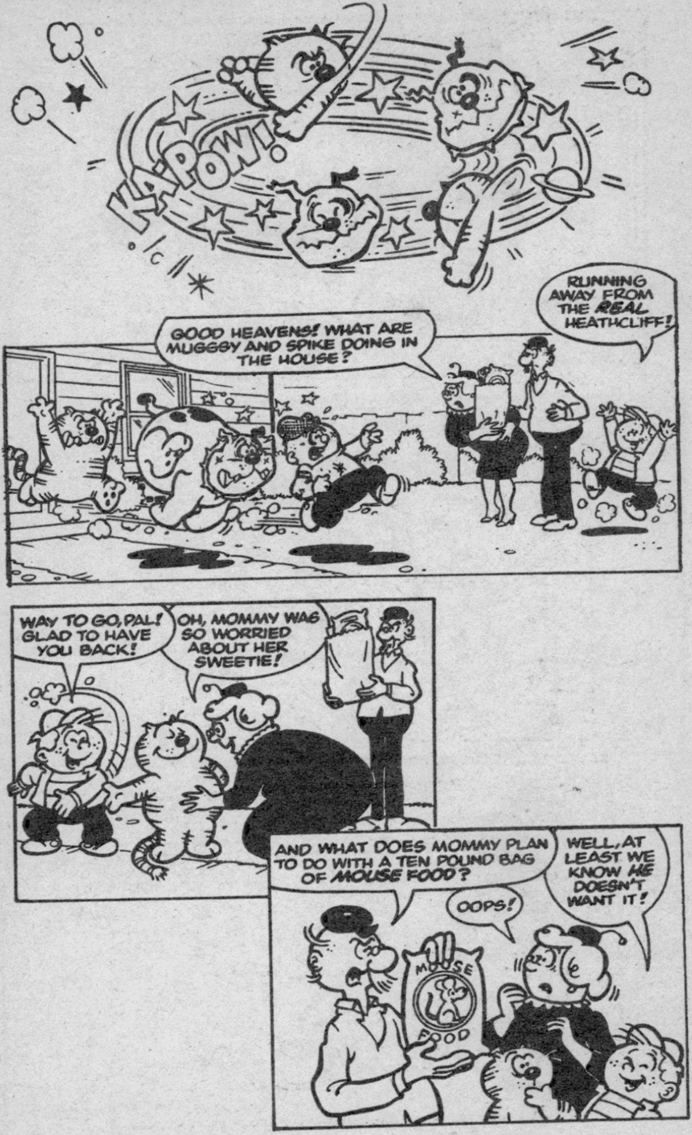
KA-POW!
GOOD HEAVENS! WHAT ARE MUGGSY AND SPIKE DOING IN THE HOUSE?
RUNNING AWAY FROM THE REAL HEATHCLIFF!
WAY TO GO, PAL! GLAD TO HAVE YOU BACK!
OH, MOMMY WAS SO WORRIED ABOUT HER SWEETIE!
AND WHAT DOES MOMMY PLAN TO DO WITH A TEN POUND BAG OF MOUSE FOOD?
OOPS!
WELL, AT LEAST WE KNOW HE DOESN'T WANT IT!
MOUSE
FOOD

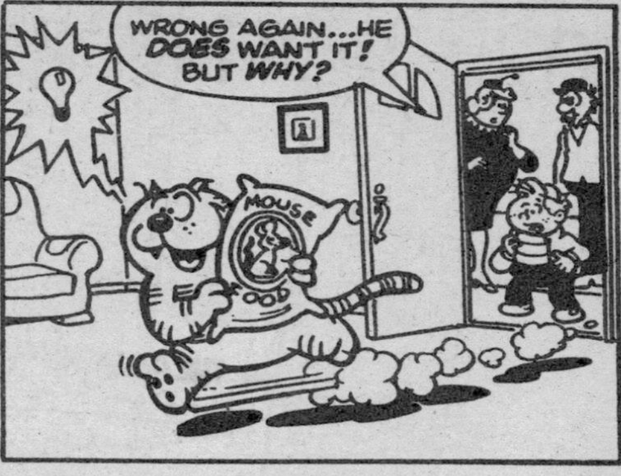
WRONG AGAIN...HE DOES WANT IT! BUT WHY?
MOUSE FOOD

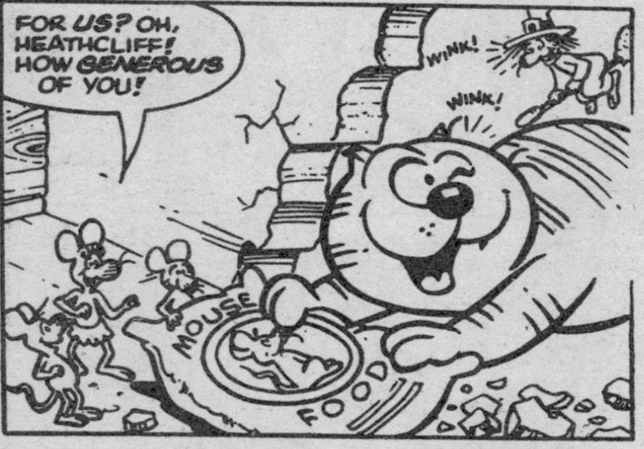
FOR US? OH, HEATHCLIFF! HOW GENEROUS OF YOU!
WINK!
WINK!
MOUSE FOOD

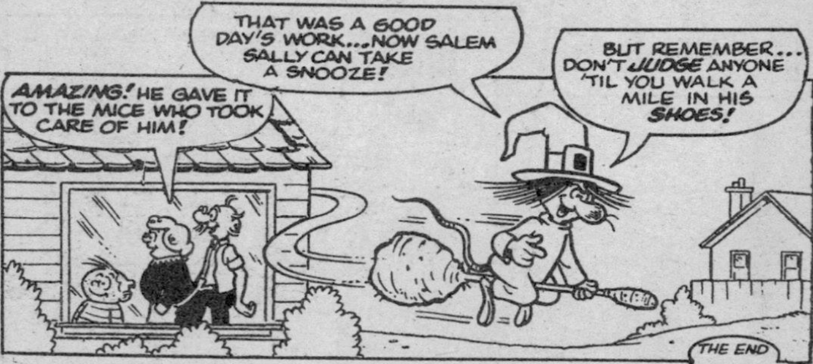
AMAZING! HE GAVE IT TO THE MICE WHO TOOK CARE OF HIM!
THAT WAS A GOOD DAY'S WORK...NOW SALEM SALLY CAN TAKE A SNOOZE!
BUT REMEMBER... DON'T JUDGE ANYONE 'TIL YOU WALK A MILE IN HIS SHOES!
THE END

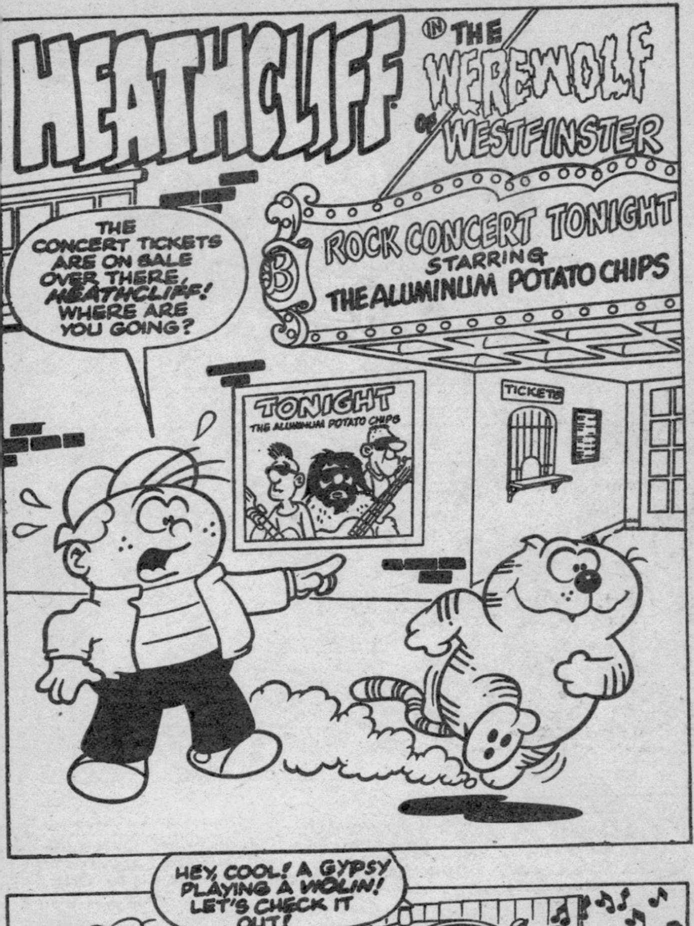
HEATHCLIFF
IN THE WEREWOLF OF WESTFINSTER
ROCK CONCERT TONIGHT
STARRING
THE ALUMINUM POTATO CHIPS
TONIGHT
THE ALUMINUM POTATO CHIPS
TICKETS
THE CONCERT TICKETS ARE ON SALE OVER THERE, HEATHCLIFF! WHERE ARE YOU GOING?

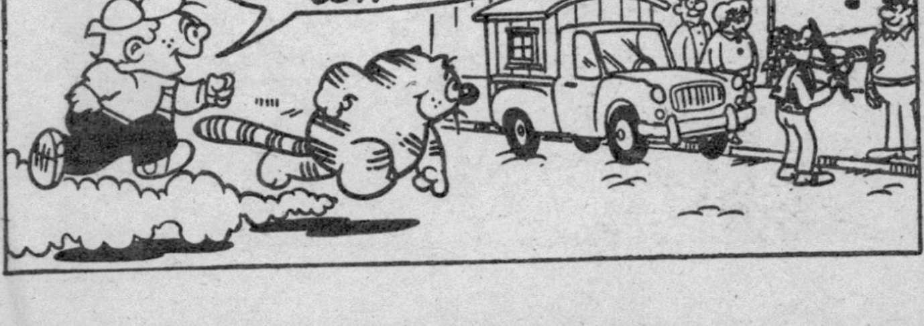
HEY, COOL! A GYPSY PLAYING A VIOLIN! LET'S CHECK IT OUT!

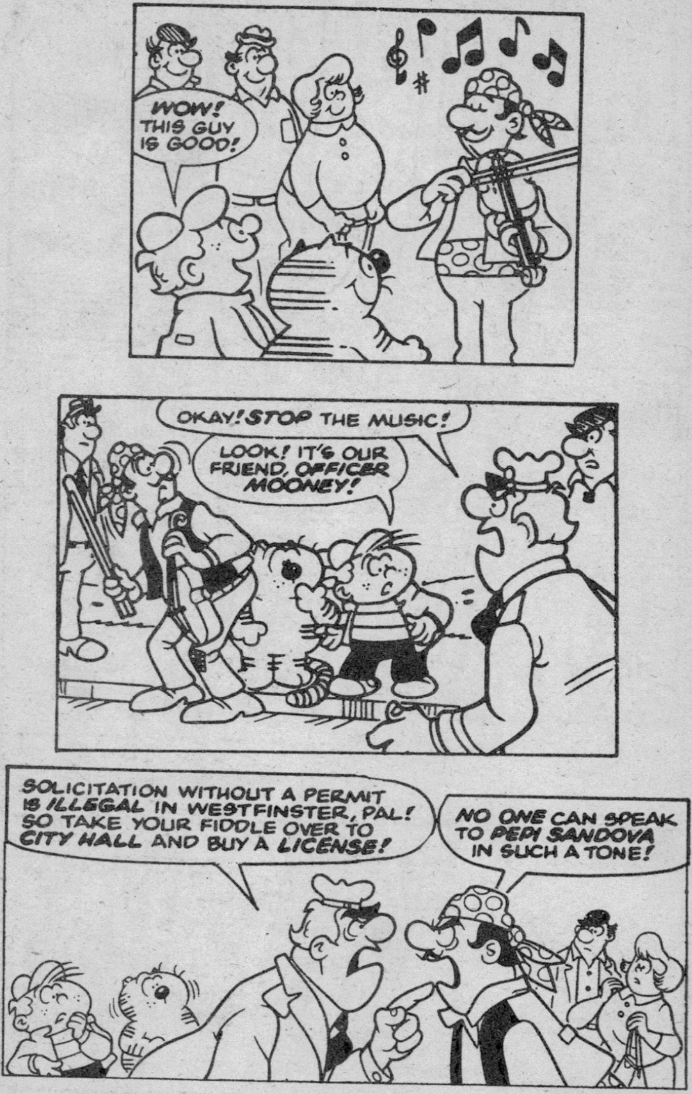
WOW! THIS GUY IS GOOD!
OKAY! STOP THE MUSIC!
LOOK! IT'S OUR FRIEND, OFFICER MOONEY!
SOLICITATION WITHOUT A PERMIT IS ILLEGAL IN WESTFINSTER, PAL! SO TAKE YOUR FIDDLE OVER TO CITY HALL AND BUY A LICENSE!
NO ONE CAN SPEAK TO PEPI SANDOVA IN SUCH A TONE!

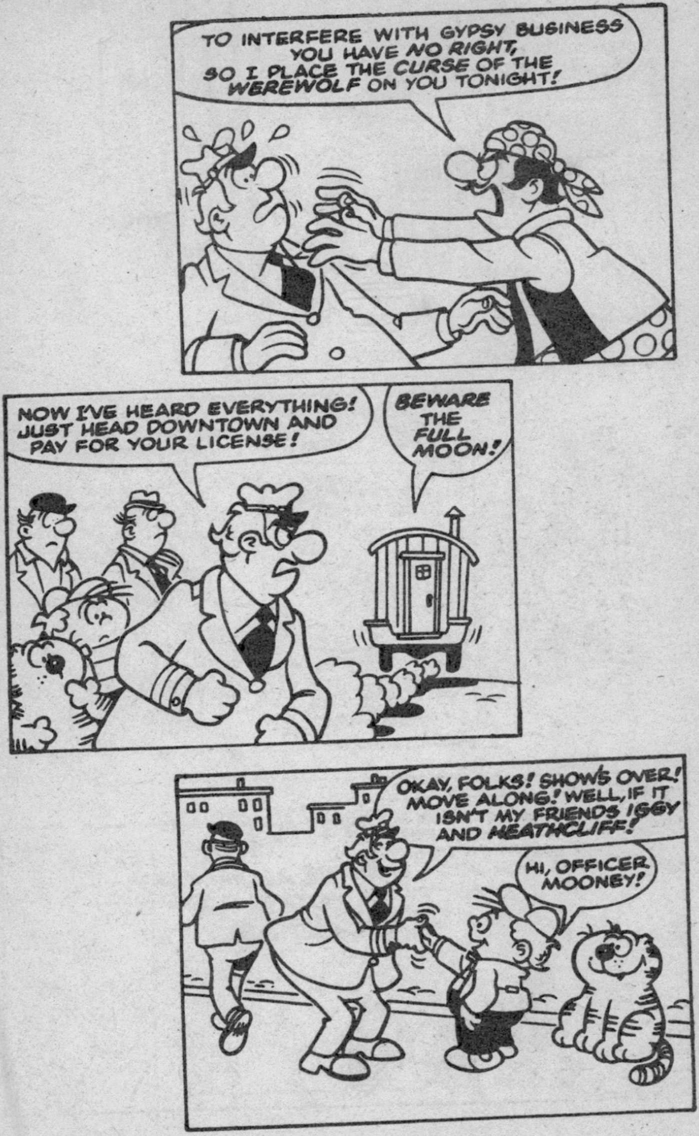
TO INTERFERE WITH GYPSY BUSINESS YOU HAVE NO RIGHT, SO I PLACE THE CURSE OF THE WEREWOLF ON YOU TONIGHT!
NOW I'VE HEARD EVERYTHING! JUST HEAD DOWNTOWN AND PAY FOR YOUR LICENSE!
BEWARE THE FULL MOON!
OKAY, FOLKS! SHOW'S OVER! MOVE ALONG! WELL, IF IT ISN'T MY FRIENDS IGGY AND HEATHCLIFF!
HI, OFFICER MOONEY!

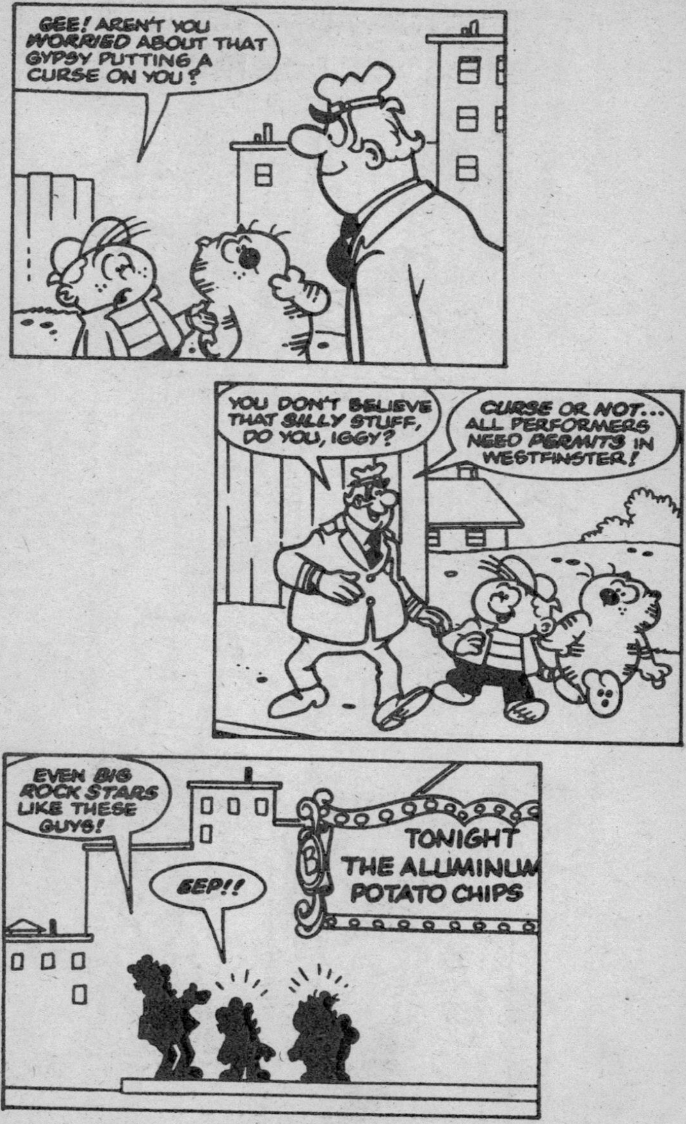
GEE! AREN'T YOU WORRIED ABOUT THAT GYPSY PUTTING A CURSE ON YOU?
YOU DON'T BELIEVE THAT SILLY STUFF, DO YOU, IGGY?
CURSE OR NOT... ALL PERFORMERS NEED PERMITS IN WESTFINSTER!
EVEN BIG ROCK STARS LIKE THESE GUYS!
EEP!!
TONIGHT THE ALUMINUM POTATO CHIPS

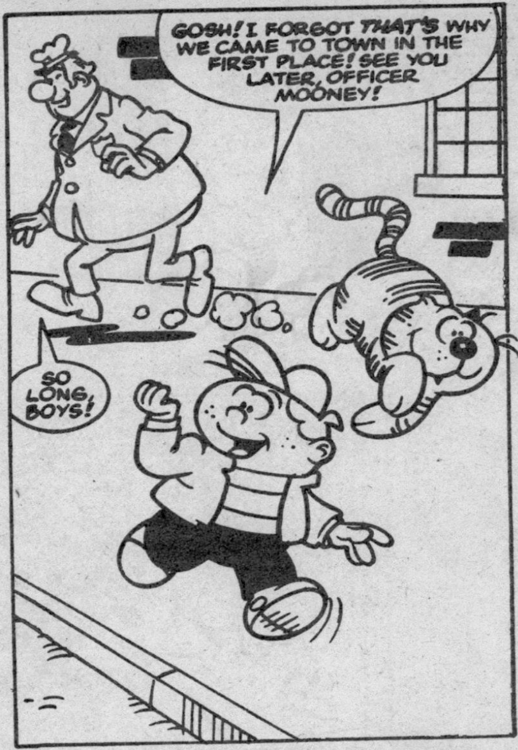
GOSH! I FORGOT THAT'S WHY WE CAME TO TOWN IN THE FIRST PLACE! SEE YOU LATER, OFFICER MOONEY!
SO LONG, BOYS!

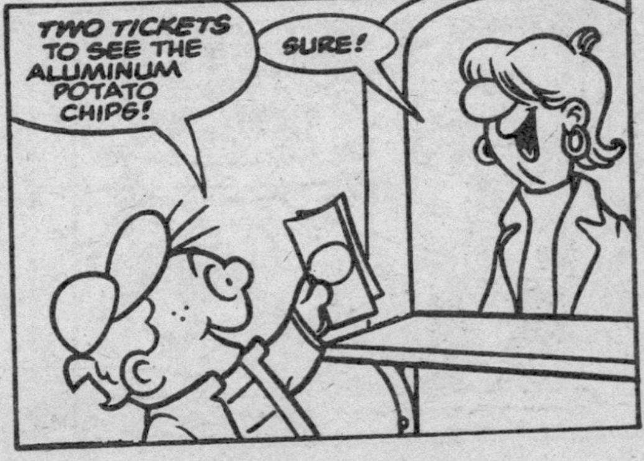
TWO TICKETS TO SEE THE ALUMINUM POTATO CHIPS!
SURE!

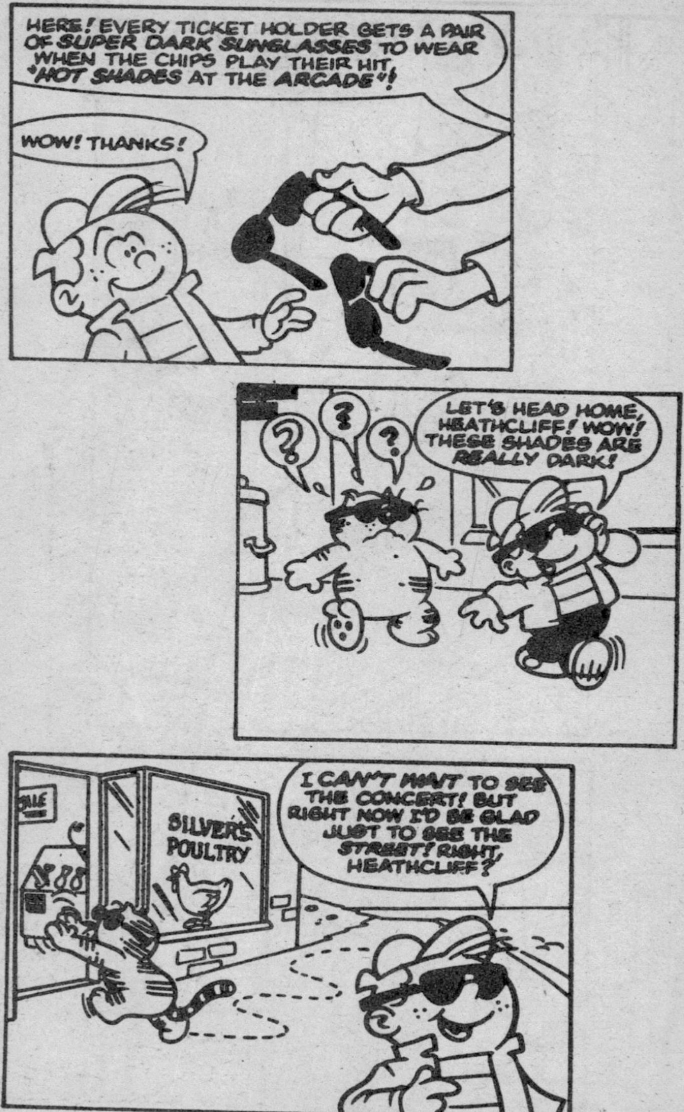
HERE! EVERY TICKET HOLDER GETS A PAIR OF SUPER DARK SUNGLASSES TO WEAR WHEN THE CHIPS PLAY THEIR HIT, "HOT SHADES AT THE ARCADE"!
WOW! THANKS!
?
?
?
LET'S HEAD HOME, HEATHCLIFF! WOW! THESE SHADES ARE REALLY DARK!
SILVER'S POULTRY
I CAN'T WAIT TO SEE THE CONCERT! BUT RIGHT NOW I'D BE GLAD JUST TO SEE THE STREET! RIGHT, HEATHCLIFF?

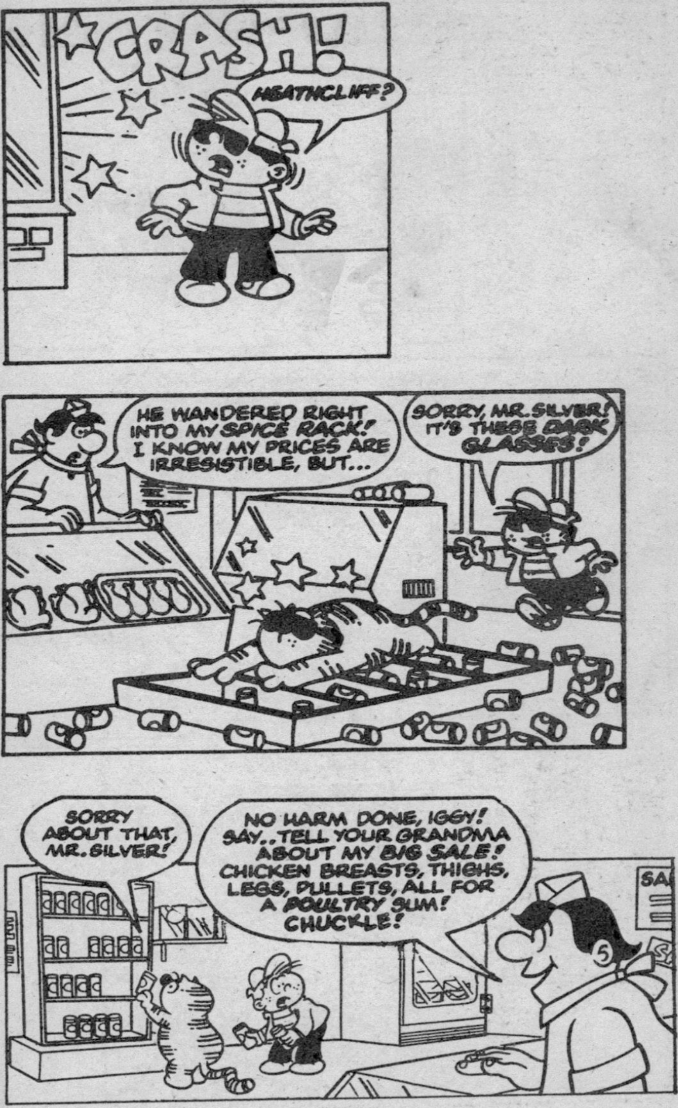
CRASH!
HEATHCLIFF?
HE WANDERED RIGHT INTO MY SPICE RACK! I KNOW MY PRICES ARE IRRESISTIBLE, BUT...
SORRY, MR. SILVER! IT'S THESE DARK GLASSES!
SORRY ABOUT THAT, MR. SILVER!
NO HARM DONE, IGGY! SAY.. TELL YOUR GRANDMA ABOUT MY BIG SALE! CHICKEN BREASTS, THIGHS, LEGS, PULLETS, ALL FOR A POULTRY SUM! CHUCKLE!

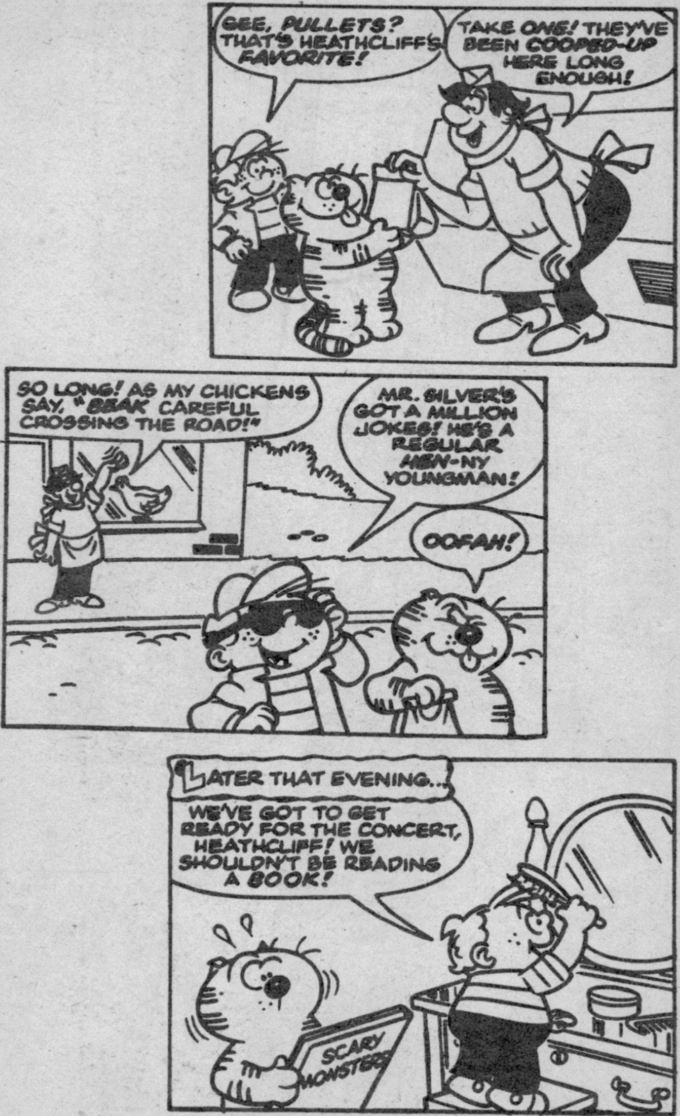
SEE, PULLETS? THAT'S HEATHCLIFF'S FAVORITE!
TAKE ONE! THEY'VE BEEN COOPED-UP HERE LONG ENOUGH!
SO LONG! AS MY CHICKENS SAY, "BEAK CAREFUL CROSSING THE ROAD!"
MR. SILVER'S GOT A MILLION JOKES! HE'S A REGULAR HEN-NY YOUNGMAN!
OOFAH!
LATER THAT EVENING...
WE'VE GOT TO GET READY FOR THE CONCERT, HEATHCLIFF! WE SHOULDN'T BE READING A BOOK!
SCARY MONSTERS

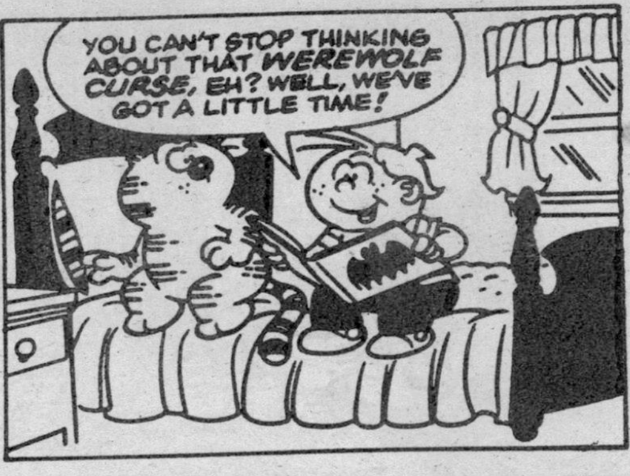
YOU CAN'T STOP THINKING ABOUT THAT WEREWOLF CURSE, EH? WELL, WE'VE GOT A LITTLE TIME!

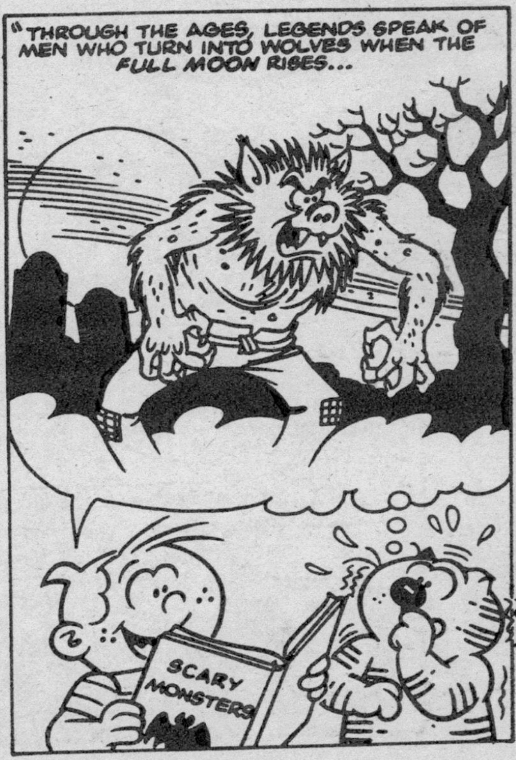
"THROUGH THE AGES, LEGENDS SPEAK OF MEN WHO TURN INTO WOLVES WHEN THE FULL MOON RISES...
SCARY MONSTERS

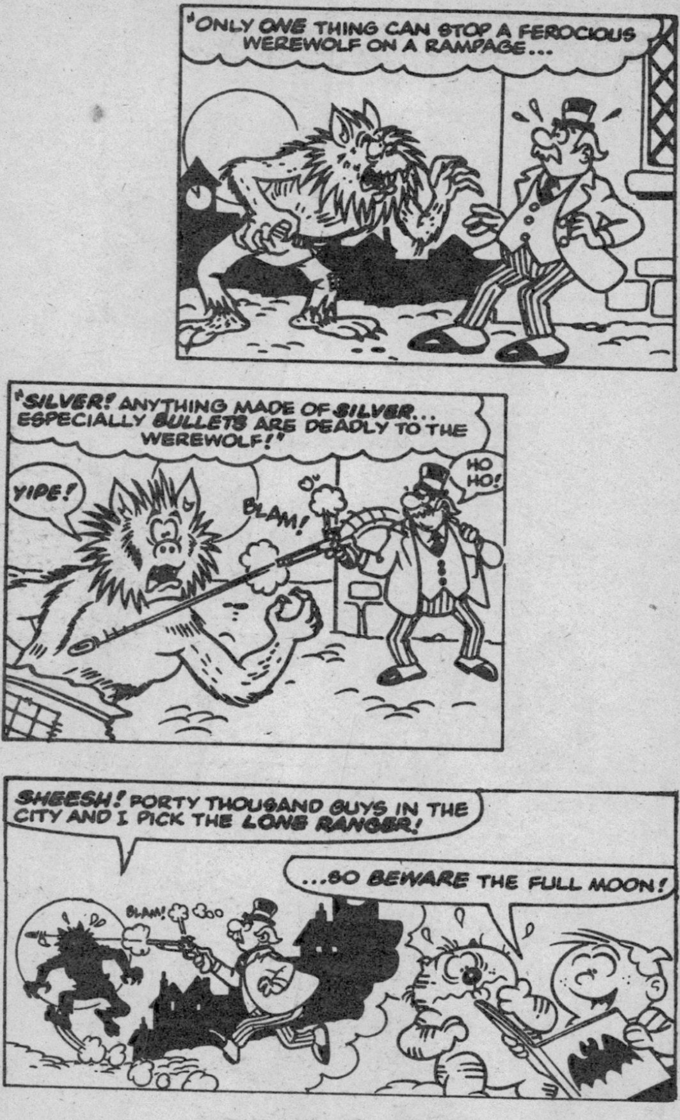
"ONLY ONE THING CAN STOP A FEROCIOUS WEREWOLF ON A RAMPAGE...
"SILVER! ANYTHING MADE OF SILVER... ESPECIALLY BULLETS ARE DEADLY TO THE WEREWOLF!"
YIPE!
BLAM!
HO HO!
SHEESH! FORTY THOUSAND GUYS IN THE CITY AND I PICK THE LONE RANGER!
BLAM!
...SO BEWARE THE FULL MOON!

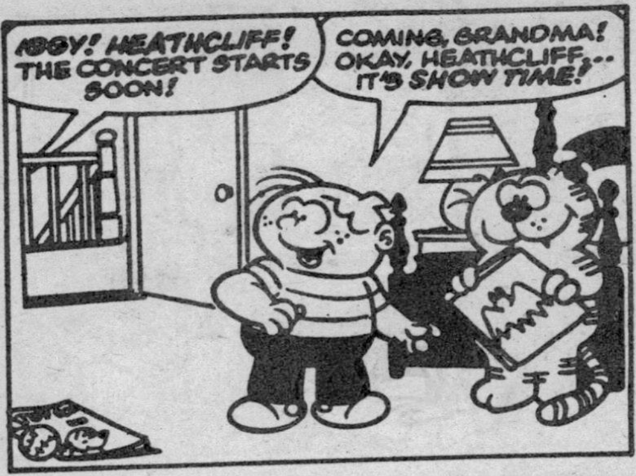
IGGY! HEATHCLIFF! THE CONCERT STARTS SOON!
COMING, GRANDMA! OKAY, HEATHCLIFF,... IT'S SHOW TIME!

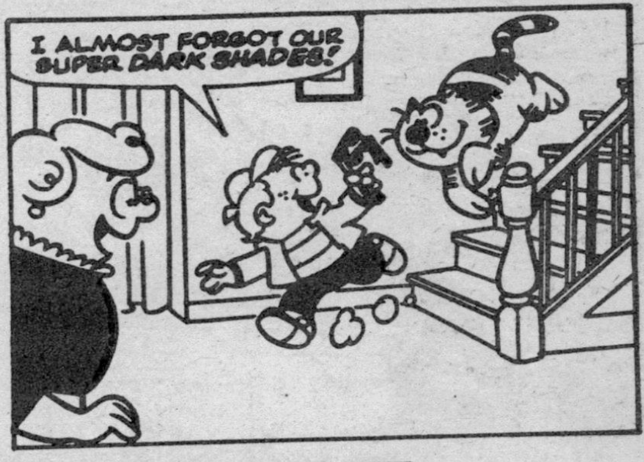
I ALMOST FORGOT OUR SUPER DARK SHADES!

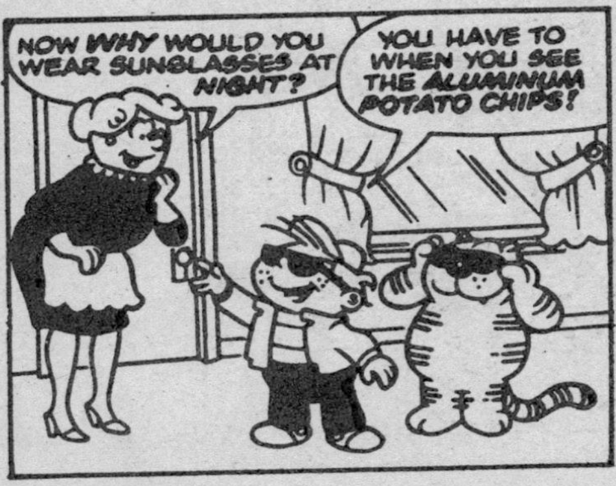
NOW WHY WOULD YOU WEAR SUNGLASSES AT NIGHT?
YOU HAVE TO WHEN YOU SEE THE ALUMINUM POTATO CHIPS!

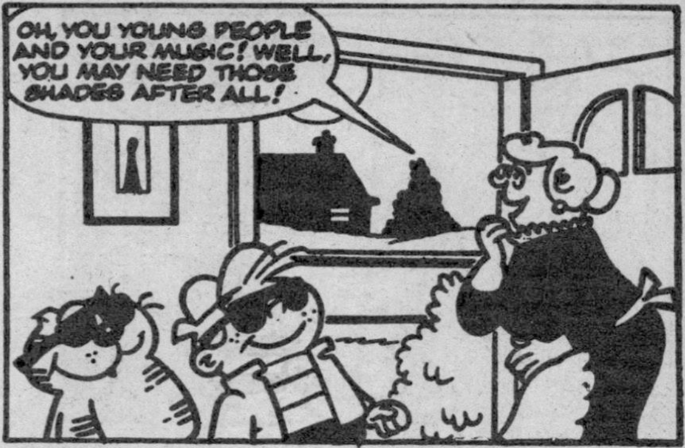
OH, YOU YOUNG PEOPLE AND YOUR MUSIC! WELL, YOU MAY NEED THOSE SHADES AFTER ALL!

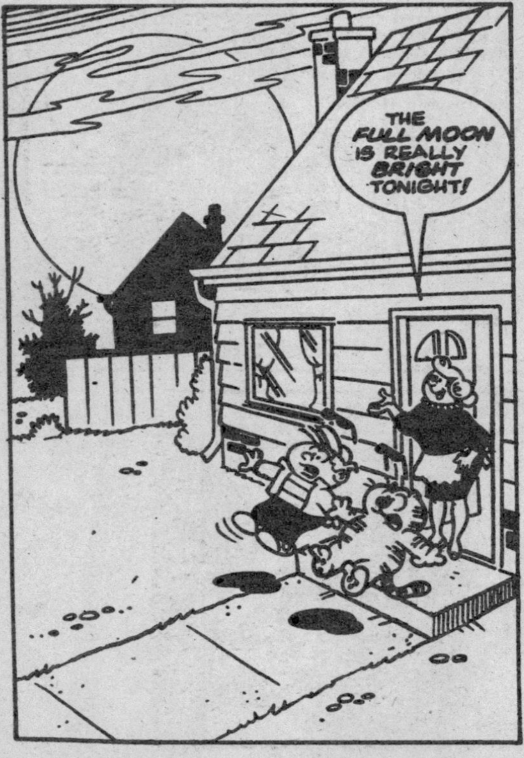
THE FULL MOON IS REALLY BRIGHT TONIGHT!

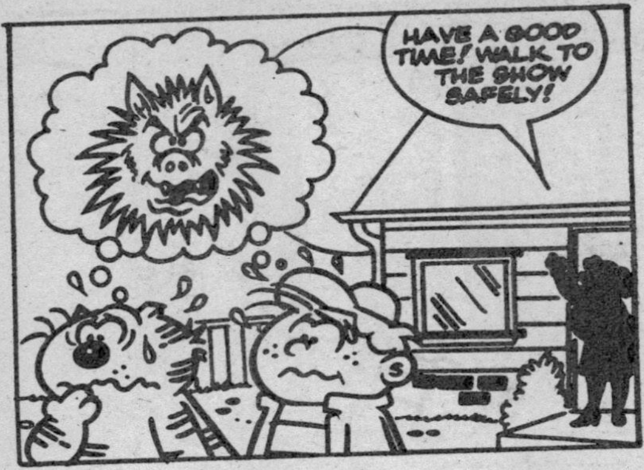
HAVE A GOOD TIME! WALK TO THE SHOW SAFELY!

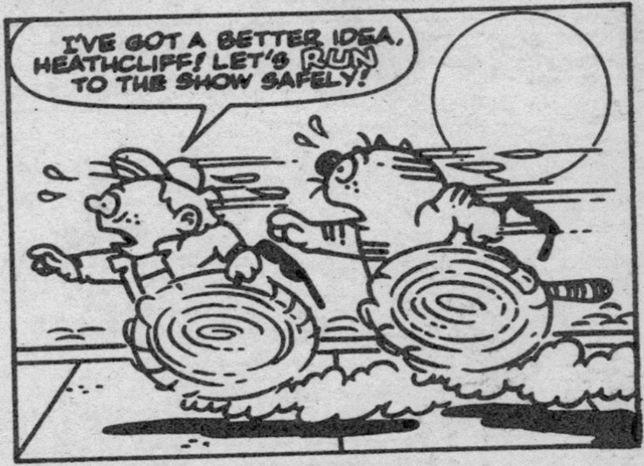
I'VE GOT A BETTER IDEA, HEATHCLIFF! LET'S RUN TO THE SHOW SAFELY!

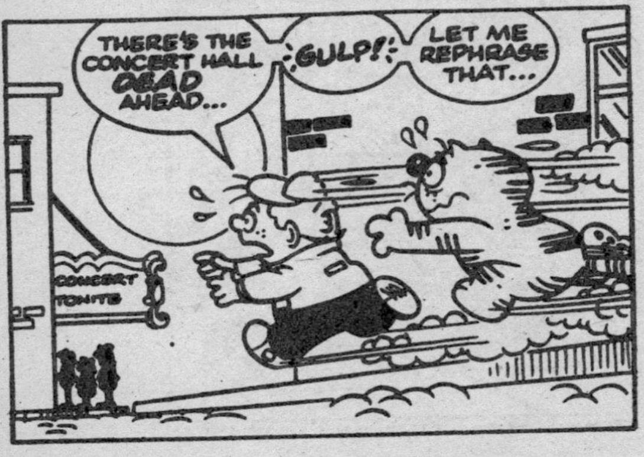
THERE'S THE CONCERT HALL DEAD AHEAD...
GULP!
LET ME REPHRASE THAT...
CONCERT
TONITE

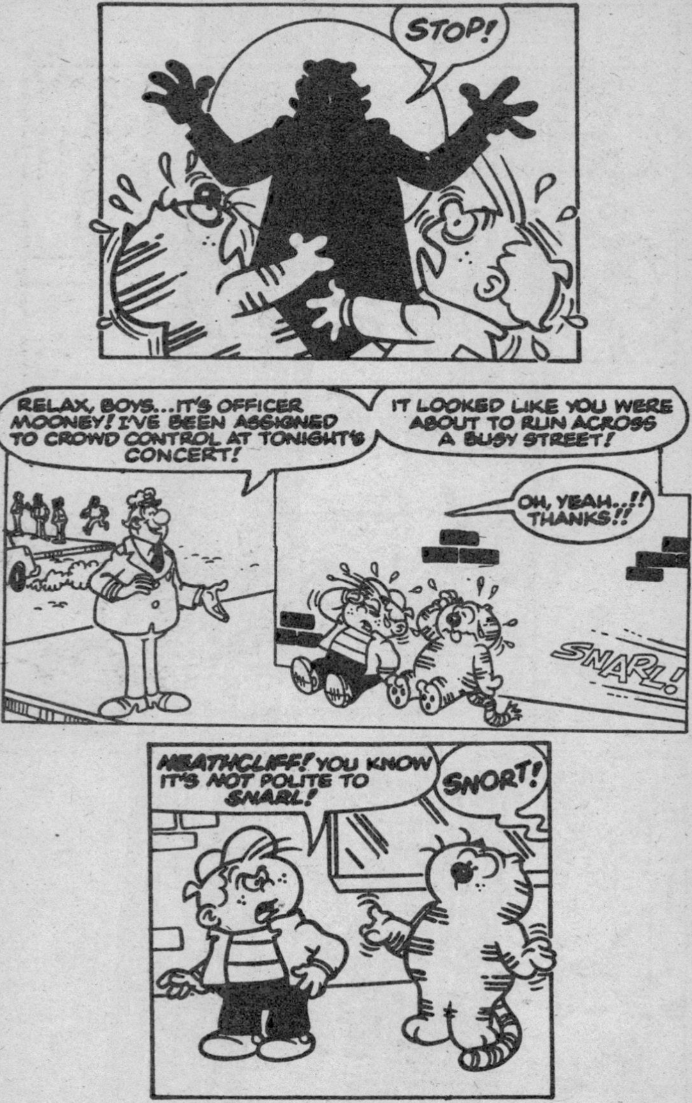
STOP!
RELAX, BOYS...IT'S OFFICER MOONEY! I'VE BEEN ASSIGNED TO CROWD CONTROL AT TONIGHT'S CONCERT!
IT LOOKED LIKE YOU WERE ABOUT TO RUN ACROSS A BUSY STREET!
OH, YEAH..!! THANKS!!
SNARL!
HEATHCLIFF! YOU KNOW IT'S NOT POLITE TO SNARL!
SNORT!

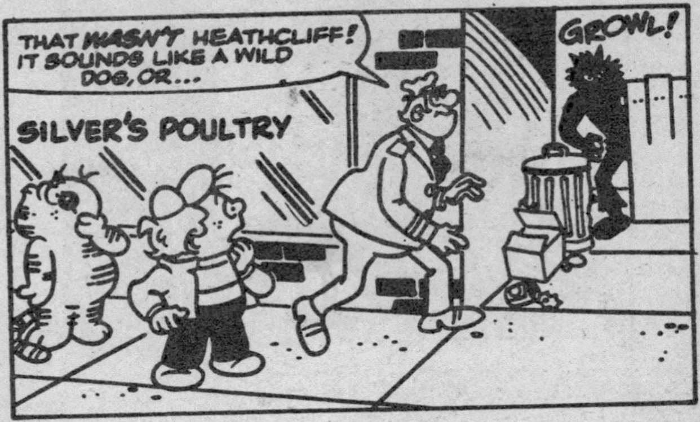
THAT WASN'T HEATHCLIFF! IT SOUNDS LIKE A WILD DOG, OR...
GROWL!
SILVER'S POULTRY

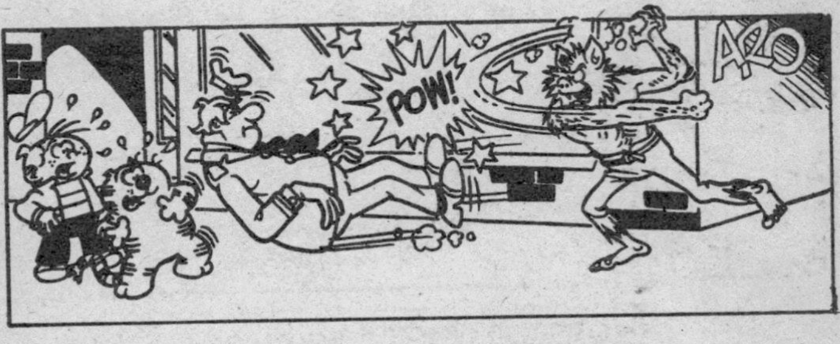
POW!
ARO

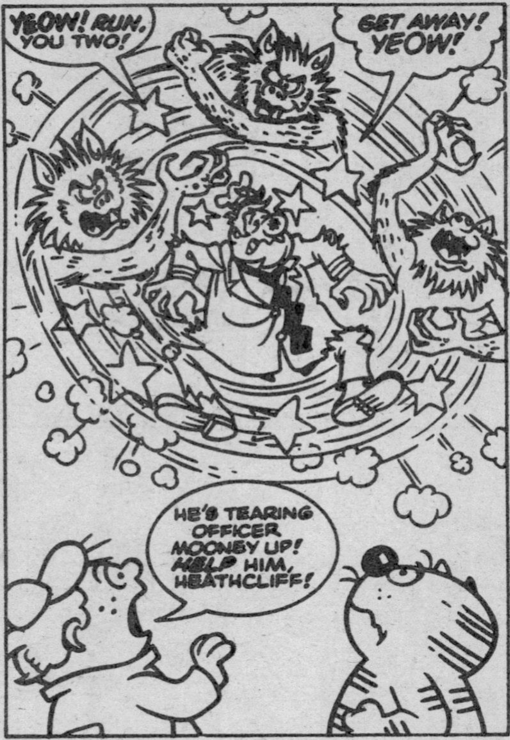
YEOW! RUN. YOU TWO!
GET AWAY! YEOW!
HE'S TEARING OFFICER MOONEY UP! HELP HIM, HEATHCLIFF!

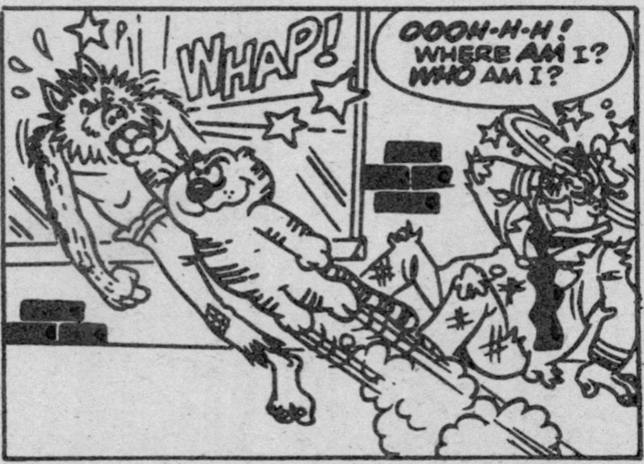
WHAP!
OOOH-H-H! WHERE AM I? WHO AM I?

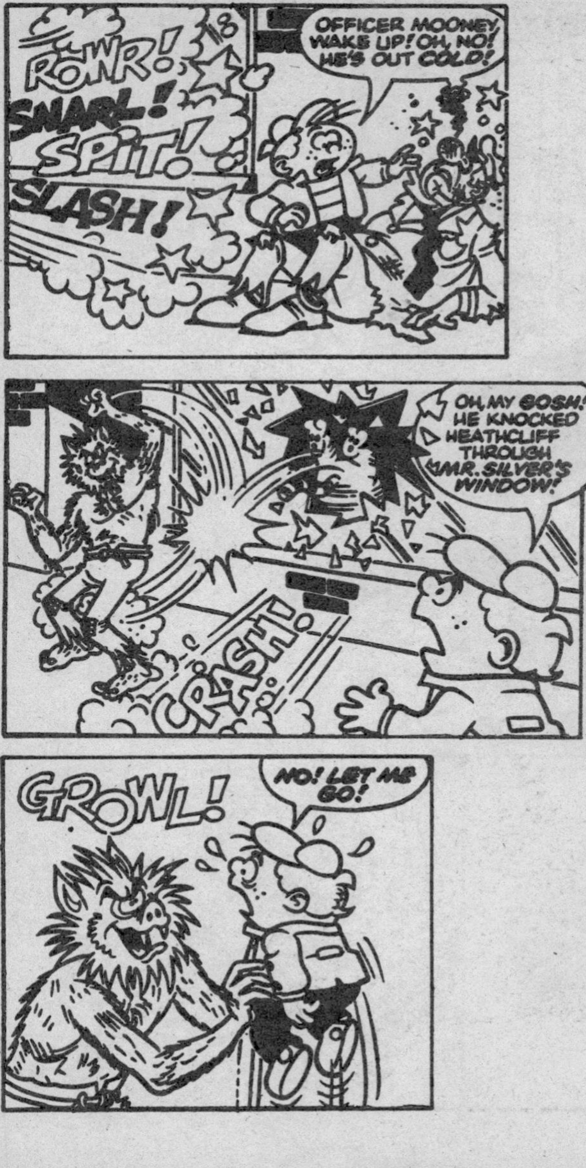
ROWR!
SNARL!
SPIT!
SLASH!
OFFICER MOONEY, WAKE UP! OH, NO! HE'S OUT COLD!
OH, MY GOSH! HE KNOCKED HEATHCLIFF THROUGH MR. SILVER'S WINDOW!
CRASH!
GROWL!
NO! LET ME GO!

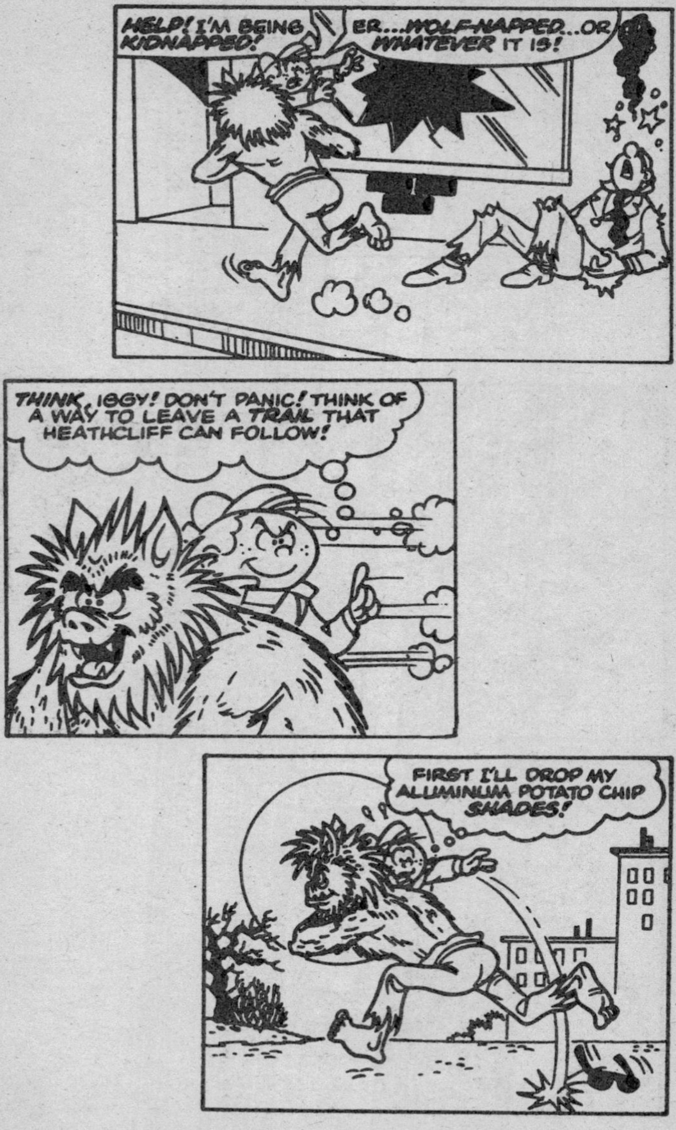
HELP! I'M BEING KIDNAPPED!
ER...WOLF-NAPPED...OR WHATEVER IT IS!
THINK, IGGY! DON'T PANIC! THINK OF A WAY TO LEAVE A TRAIL THAT HEATHCLIFF CAN FOLLOW!
FIRST I'LL DROP MY ALUMINUM POTATO CHIP SHADES!

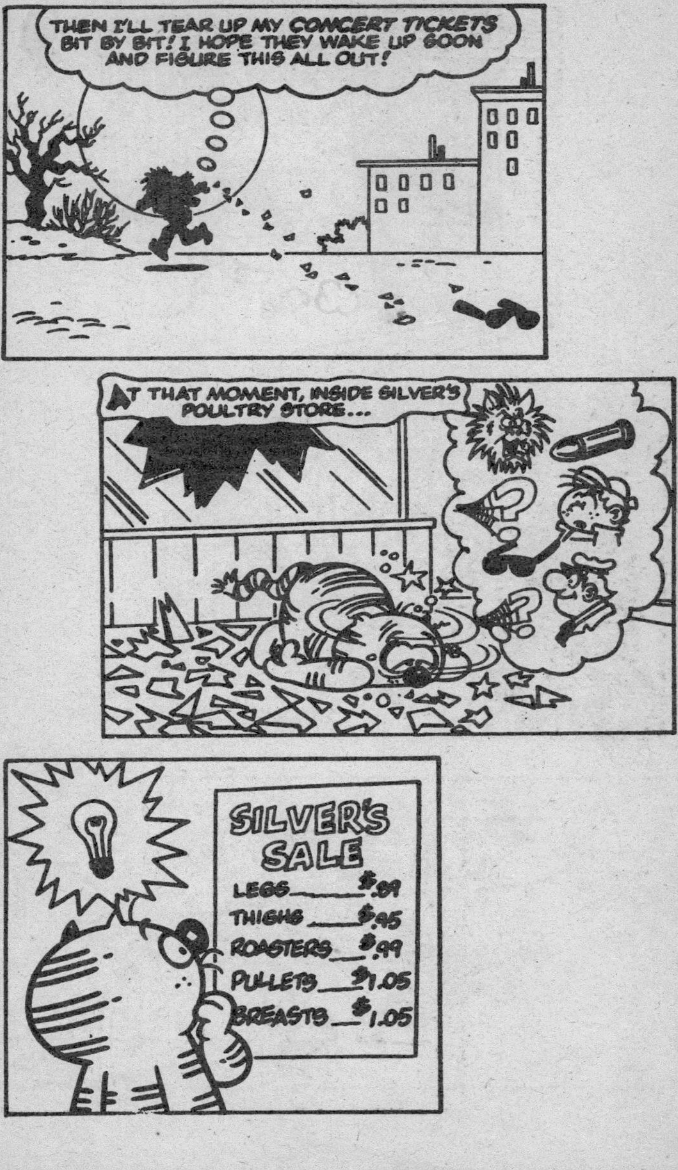
THEN I'LL TEAR UP MY CONCERT TICKETS BIT BY BIT! I HOPE THEY WAKE UP SOON AND FIGURE THIS ALL OUT!
AT THAT MOMENT, INSIDE SILVER'S POULTRY STORE...
SILVER'S SALE
LEGS ___ $.89
THIGHS ___ $.95
ROASTERS ___ $.99
PULLETS ___ $1.05
BREASTS ___ $1.05

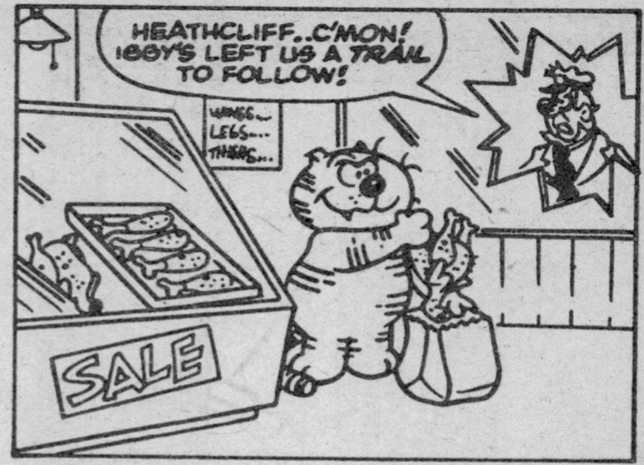
HEATHCLIFF..C'MON! IGGY'S LEFT US A *TRAIL* TO FOLLOW!
WINGS...
LEGS...
THIGHS...
SALE

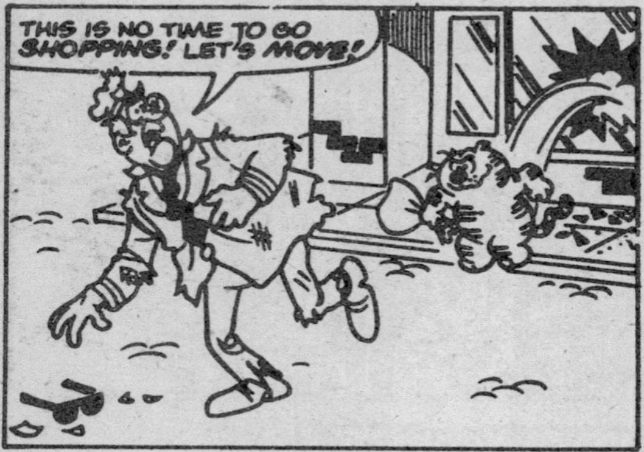
THIS IS NO TIME TO GO *SHOPPING!* LET'S *MOVE!*

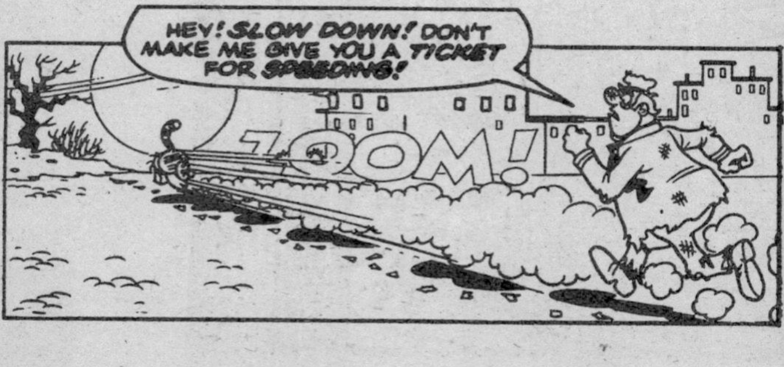
HEY! *SLOW DOWN!* DON'T MAKE ME GIVE YOU A *TICKET* FOR *SPEEDING!*
ZOOM!

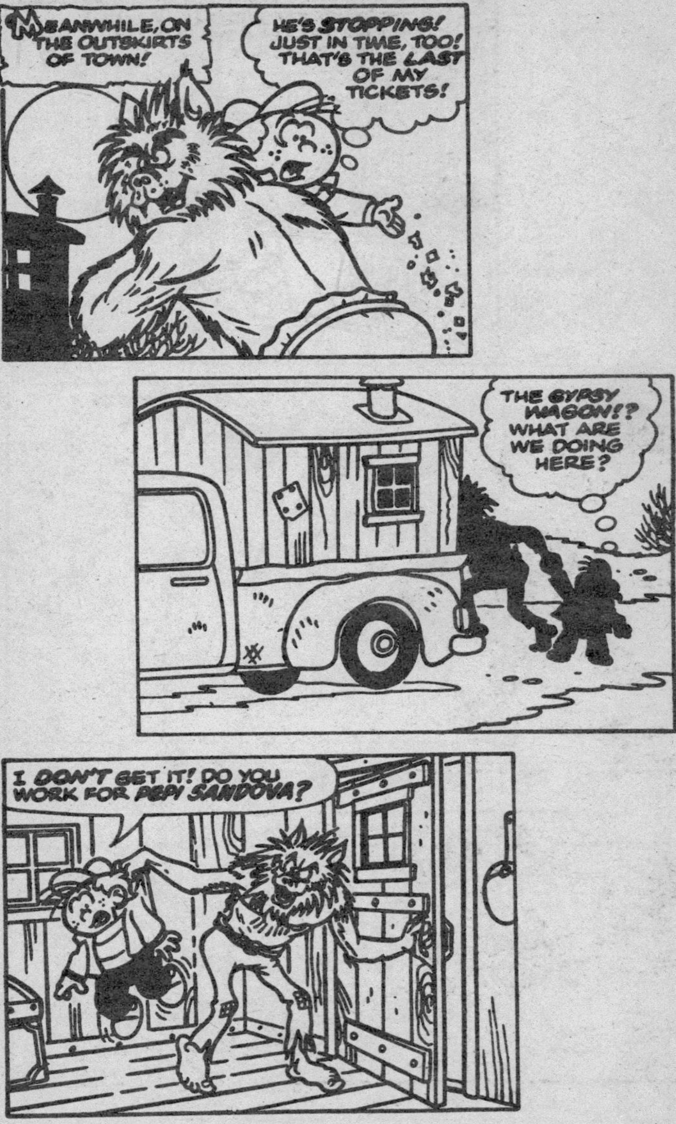
MEANWHILE, ON THE OUTSKIRTS OF TOWN!
HE'S *STOPPING!* JUST IN TIME, TOO! THAT'S THE *LAST* OF MY TICKETS!
THE *GYPSY WAGON!?* WHAT ARE WE DOING HERE?
I *DON'T* GET IT! DO YOU WORK FOR *PEPI SANDOVA?*

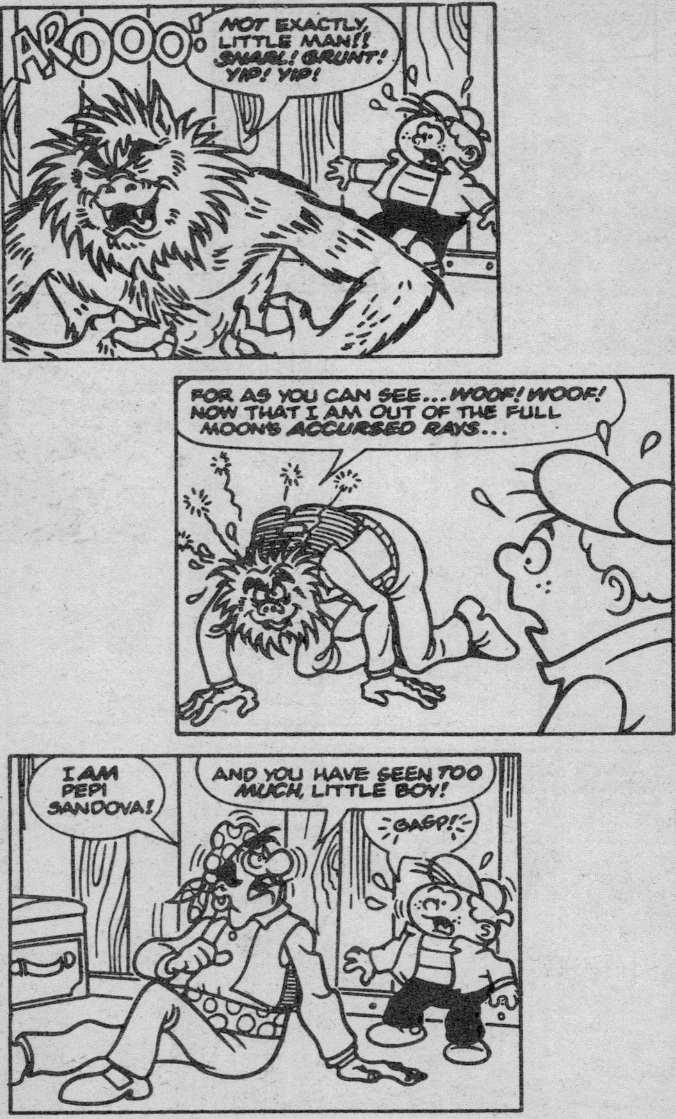
AROOOO!
NOT EXACTLY, LITTLE MAN!! SNARL! GRUNT! YIP! YIP!
FOR AS YOU CAN SEE... WOOF! WOOF! NOW THAT I AM OUT OF THE FULL MOON'S ACCURSED RAYS...
I AM PEPI SANDOVA!
AND YOU HAVE SEEN TOO MUCH, LITTLE BOY!
GASP!

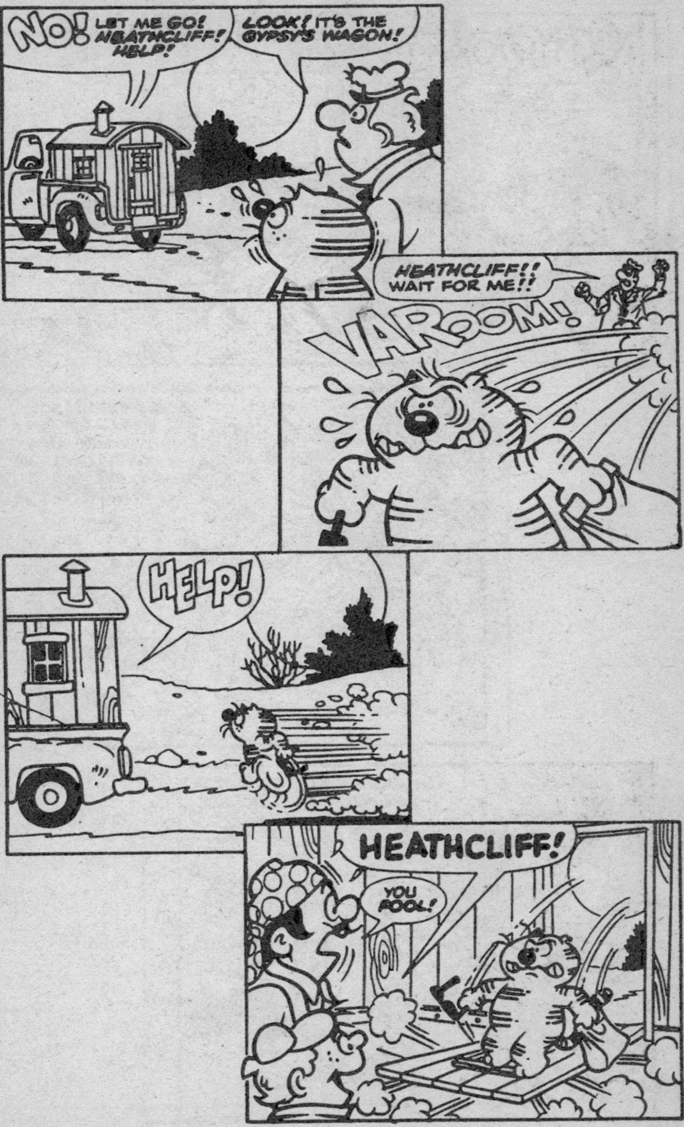
NO! LET ME GO! HEATHCLIFF! HELP!
LOOK! IT'S THE GYPSY'S WAGON!
HEATHCLIFF!! WAIT FOR ME!!
VAROOM!
HELP!
HEATHCLIFF!
YOU FOOL!

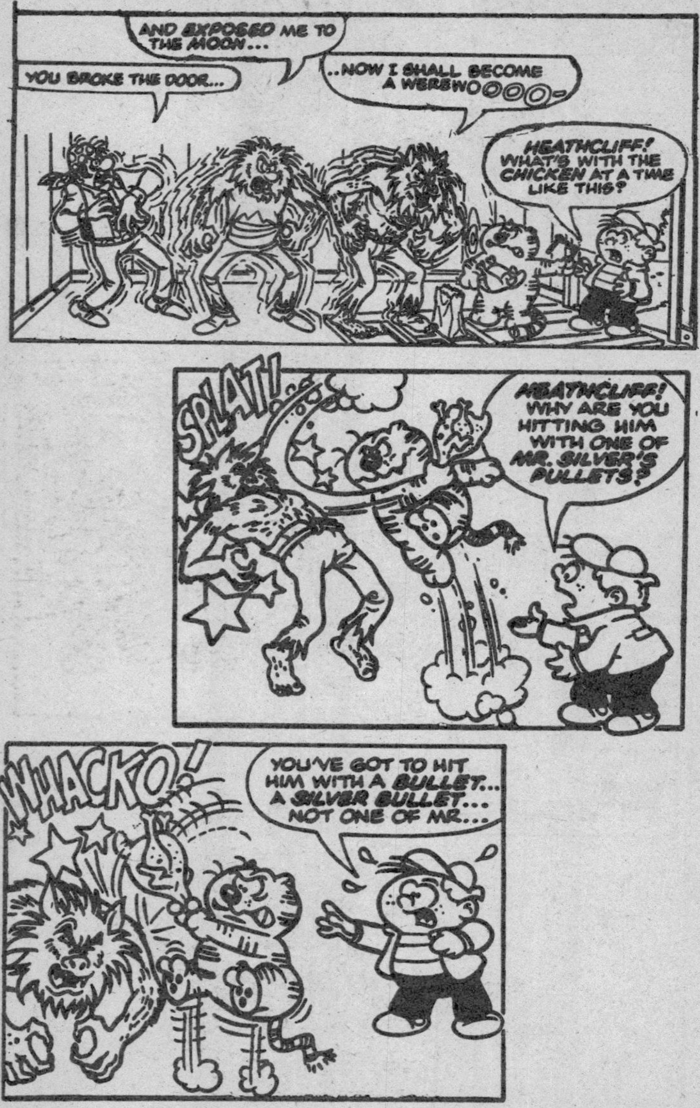
YOU BROKE THE DOOR...
AND EXPOSED ME TO THE MOON...
...NOW I SHALL BECOME A WEREWOOOO-
HEATHCLIFF! WHAT'S WITH THE CHICKEN AT A TIME LIKE THIS?
SPLAT!
HEATHCLIFF! WHY ARE YOU HITTING HIM WITH ONE OF MR. SILVER'S PULLETS?
WHACKO!
YOU'VE GOT TO HIT HIM WITH A BULLET... A SILVER BULLET... NOT ONE OF MR...

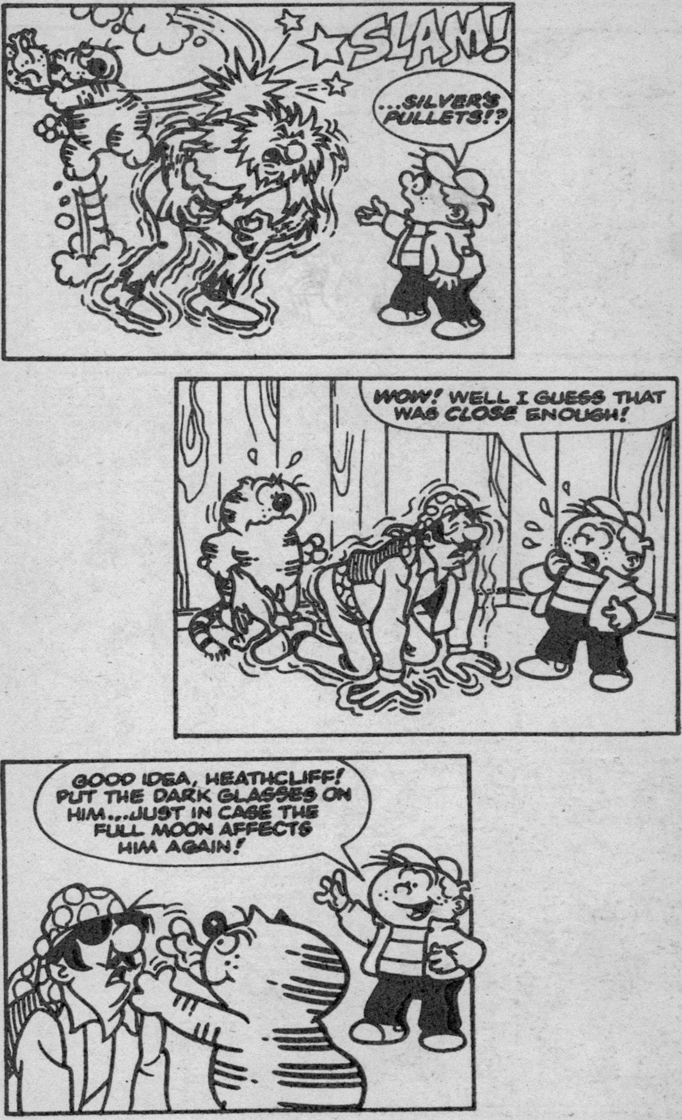
SLAM!
...SILVER'S PULLETS!?
WOW! WELL I GUESS THAT WAS CLOSE ENOUGH!
GOOD IDEA, HEATHCLIFF! PUT THE DARK GLASSES ON HIM...JUST IN CASE THE FULL MOON AFFECTS HIM AGAIN!

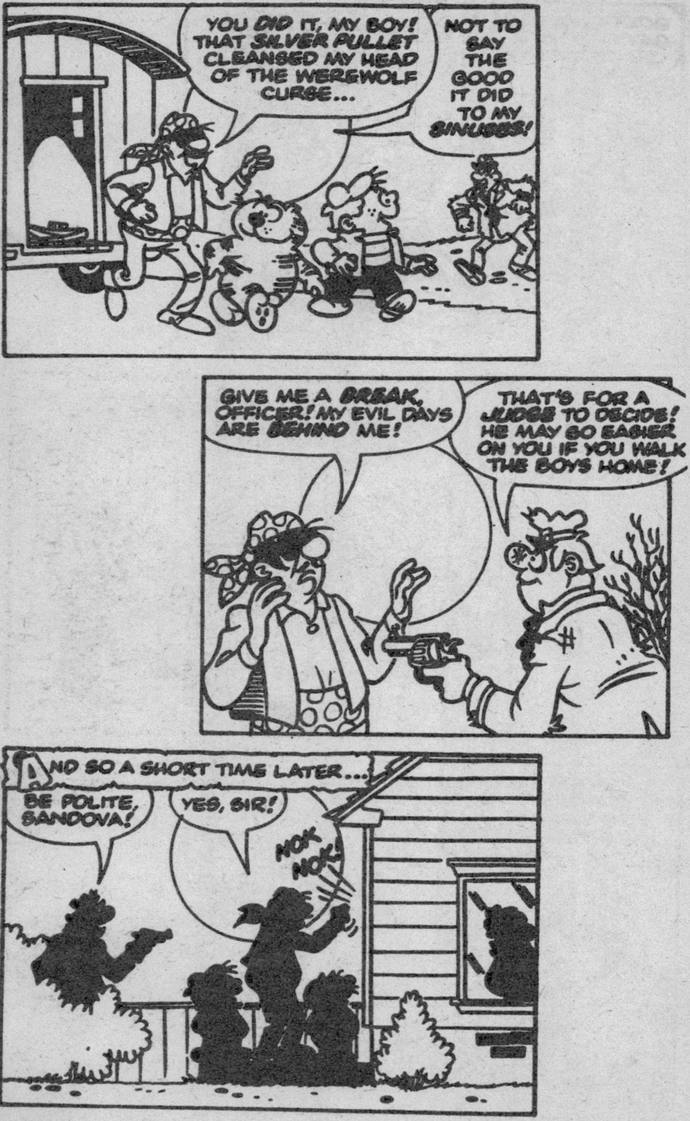
YOU DID IT, MY BOY! THAT SILVER PULLET CLEANSED MY HEAD OF THE WEREWOLF CURSE...
NOT TO SAY THE GOOD IT DID TO MY SINUSES!
GIVE ME A BREAK, OFFICER! MY EVIL DAYS ARE BEHIND ME!
THAT'S FOR A JUDGE TO DECIDE! HE MAY GO EASIER ON YOU IF YOU WALK THE BOYS HOME!
AND SO A SHORT TIME LATER...
BE POLITE, SANDOVA!
YES, SIR!
NOK NOK

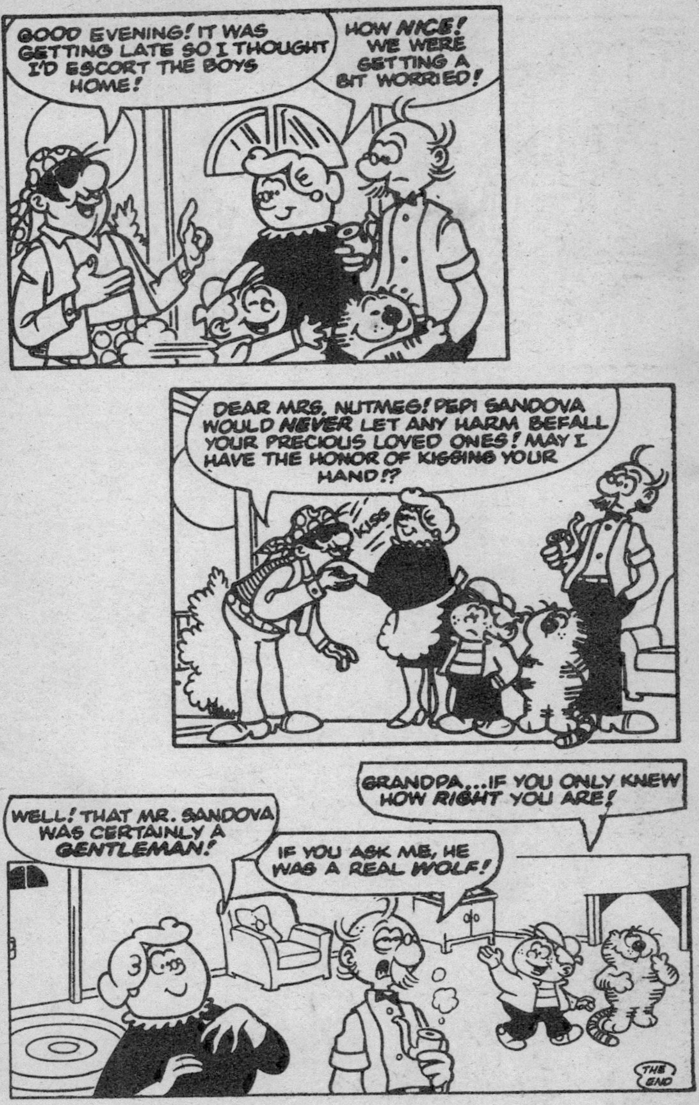
GOOD EVENING! IT WAS GETTING LATE SO I THOUGHT I'D ESCORT THE BOYS HOME!
HOW NICE! WE WERE GETTING A BIT WORRIED!
DEAR MRS. NUTMEG! PEPI SANDOVA WOULD NEVER LET ANY HARM BEFALL YOUR PRECIOUS LOVED ONES! MAY I HAVE THE HONOR OF KISSING YOUR HAND!?
KISS
WELL! THAT MR. SANDOVA WAS CERTAINLY A GENTLEMAN!
IF YOU ASK ME, HE WAS A REAL WOLF!
GRANDPA...IF YOU ONLY KNEW HOW RIGHT YOU ARE!
THE END

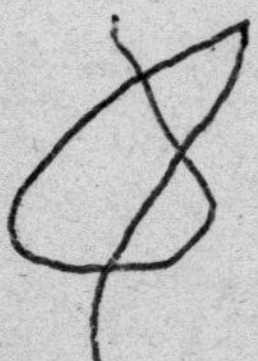